RITUALS
FOR
LIFE

FIND MEANING
IN YOUR
EVERYDAY MOMENTS

MEERA LESTER

ADAMS MEDIA
NEW YORK   LONDON   TORONTO   SYDNEY   NEW DELHI

Adams Media
An Imprint of Simon & Schuster, Inc.
57 Littlefield Street
Avon, Massachusetts 02322

First Adams Media hardcover edition DECEMBER 2017

ADAMS MEDIA and colophon are trademarks of Simon and Schuster.

For information about special discounts for bulk purchases, please contact Simon & Schuster Special Sales at 1-866-506-1949 or business@simonandschuster.com.

The Simon & Schuster Speakers Bureau can bring authors to your live event. For more information or to book an event contact the Simon & Schuster Speakers Bureau at 1-866-248-3049 or visit our website at www.simonspeakers.com.

Interior design by Michelle Kelly

Manufactured in the United States of America

10 9 8 7 6 5 4 3 2 1

Library of Congress Cataloging-in-Publication Data
Lester, Meera, author.
Rituals for life / Meera Lester.
Avon, Massachusetts: Adams Media, 2017.
LCCN 2017032773 (print) | LCCN 2017043319 (ebook) | ISBN 9781507205242 (hc) | ISBN 9781507205259 (ebook)
LCSH: Mind and body. | Mind and body therapies--Popular works. | Well-being.
LCC BF161 (ebook) | LCC BF161 .L435 2017 (print) | DDC 158.1--dc23
LC record available at https://lccn.loc.gov/2017032773

ISBN 978-1-5072-0524-2
ISBN 978-1-5072-0525-9 (ebook)

Contents

Chapter 8: Rituals for a More Grounded You 159

INTRODUCTION

Rituals, or repetitive acts, already fill our lives. Some have become so common—our morning cup of coffee, friendly hugs hello, afternoon walks—that we hardly pay attention to them. However, even the most ordinary repetitive act can add meaning to your life.

You will soon discover how to transform everyday activities into mindfulness exercises. By instilling purpose into your actions, you will be able to rely on them as a means of self-fortitude, drawing on these rituals to feel centered, connected, and grounded. The intention of this book is to help you become more aware of your actions, turn them into rituals, and give them a richness that makes them even more meaningful.

From the moment you wake up until the time you go to bed, there are a number of opportunities to empower everything you do. Some of the suggestions included in this book deal with self-reflection for a sound mind, others promote perfecting your physical health, and some look to strengthen your connections to the people around you.

You will be able to use these ideas individually, or learn how to create purposeful routines to enhance your well-being and structure your day. When you find the right pattern of rituals in your life, you feel fulfilled, nourished, and on track with your destiny. The rituals outlined in the following chapters—and whatever others you may evolve in the future after you're comfortable with these—are a way for you to take time to create meaning and purpose today and every day.

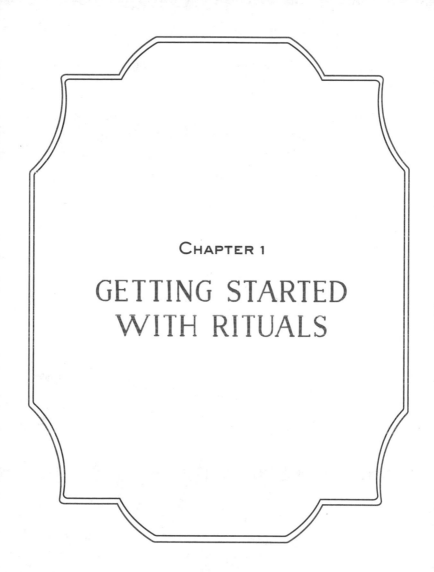

CHAPTER 1

GETTING STARTED WITH RITUALS

Whether you participate in a ritual alone or with a group, by engaging in it you are taking part in an activity that is filled with emotions—pride, happiness, serenity, and so forth. These may be simple or complex, but in either case your actions make you look at the world differently and find strength within yourself. Sometimes a ritual helps you calm down; if you're scared of something, the ritual can give you courage. Some rituals fill you with pride and happiness.

Rituals can include:

- Marriages and funerals
- Civil ceremonies (e.g., being inducted into the armed forces)
- Rites of passage (e.g., birthdays, graduation from college)
- Worship
- Meditation
- Cleansing and purification
- Birthing and baptism
- Naming

Often we perform rituals because we expect a particular outcome—reassurance, strength, renewed hope, support, control, relief from pressure and stress, and a stronger sense of belonging. We perform rituals for an audience even if that audience is only ourselves. Rituals inspire dreams, spark creative vision, suggest new paths, and offer healing. They help us explore new places within ourselves and others.

OBJECTS IN YOUR RITUALS

You don't have to use an object for your ritual, but for some, one can be helpful. You might want to use an item that speaks to you through its sound, taste, or scent. From the scent of fresh flowers and the taste of warming spices to the sound of bells and the tactile reassurance of crystals, you can use a number of different items in your ceremony.

HOW TO USE THIS BOOK

In each suggested ritual, you'll find general information including an intended benefit of doing the ritual. You will also find suggestions on how to make the ceremony more meaningful. How much time you take to perform the ritual and when during the day or night you do it is up to you. The only person who can decide how to fit one or more rituals in your life is you. The rituals offered in this book are fairly generic; make them yours by using imagination and creativity to add to them or envisioning new ones.

At the end of each chapter there are some suggested sequences for some of the rituals. These are designed to help you, but you may prefer to develop your own sequences. The rituals can work together to reinforce and enhance one another, and the sequences will help you with this.

Through rituals you can give meaning to your life, in both the big, exciting moments and the small, ordinary ones. Use rituals to discover the secrets you keep inside yourself. In this way, you can bring joy in every moment of your day.

CHAPTER 2

RITUALS FOR A HEALTHIER YOU

Vibrant mind-body health is a treasure to be safeguarded to the last breath. Without robust health, how can you achieve peak performance or optimal functioning in any other area of your life? Perhaps you already do a daily workout as well as eat nutritious foods, stay hydrated, and get adequate sleep. For maximum health benefits, add mindfulness to transform a routine into a ritual. Perhaps the simplest practice that you can do is to simply stop and just be. While you are physically still and mindful, notice how your senses communicate your body's aliveness.

Mindfulness adds to your routines the benefit of improved memory, stable hormonal balance, a stronger immune system, less pain, lower blood pressure, and better sleep. Mindfulness anchors you in the here and now, which means you are living in the moment, not obsessing about the past or worrying about the future.

In addition to adopting some of the rituals in this chapter, you might try asking a question in your heart space for guidance about your body's health and then listen for the answer. It's been often repeated that the body has wisdom of its own. A body that is energetic, mentally sharp, and emotionally stable and happy is communicating good health. When something isn't right, you know it. Mindfulness enables you to tune into the signs.

RITUAL 1.
GREET THE DAWN

AWAKEN YOUR VIBES AS YOU
AWAKEN TO THE DAY

Studies show that early risers are healthier, happier, and more productive than their night owl counterparts. Waking up early doesn't mean you must leap out of bed. Before throwing off those covers to drink water, attend to hygiene, exercise, and eat breakfast, take some time to linger in that quiet space between sleeping and wakefulness with a morning ritual that focuses on gathering in positive energy. Don't rush from this quiet in-between state known as the hypnopompic state. Like its counterpart, the hypnagogic state (between wakefulness and sleep), it holds for you gifts of extraordinary phenomena, including:

- Intense imagery
- Audible sounds of nature, voices, and music
- Taste sensations
- Touch sensitivity
- Otherworldly scents of incense or florals or unidentifiable smells
- A heightened sense of presence

Since ancient times, yogis have hailed the hour and a half before sunrise as the most auspicious time of the day. Some believe that accessing the positivity and power of deeper meditative states is easier in the predawn when your mind is still. Keep a small stone by your bedside. Hold it on awakening to remind you to generate positive vibes from this time and take them with you into your day.

RITUAL 2.
DO DEEP BREATHING

ANCHOR YOUR MIND TO GREET
YOUR ESSENTIAL SELF

From the moment you awaken your mind begins chattering with a steady stream of thoughts. Establish a positive mental state by counting a cycle of deep and slow breaths for five minutes or more. Make the count of your exhalation twice as long as the inhalation. Or do your favorite *pranayama* (breath control). Mindful breath work is a surefire way to calm the noise in your mind, slow the mental babble, and center your thoughts. Deep breathing can be done anytime during the day when you have a free minute or two.

Before an early-morning ritual of breath work, note the following:

- Avoid eating for several hours (easy when you do your practice upon awakening)
- Drink only water one half-hour before practice
- Wear loose clothes
- Align your head and spine for correct posture

Eating and drinking can cause stomach upset and you don't want your clothes to bind you as practice deep breathing.

Deep breathing detoxifies your body and oxygenates your cells while easing away stress and tension. It strengthens the lungs, heart, and immune system and also elevates mood, boosts stamina, and generates mental acuity. The mind follows the breath. As when the breeze stops its agitation of the lake and the surface becomes calm and transparent, similarly, your mind when anchored in mindful breathing achieves clarity with the power to reflect your essential Self.

RITUAL 3.
CHANT

Invoke the Power
of Positive Energy

Chanting possesses a potency that empowers you to feel more joyful, relaxed, focused, and on purpose with your life. Your spiritual energy centers (chakras) and life-force energy (prana) become supercharged with positive vibrations during a chanting session. Studies in neuro science suggest that chanting blocks the release of stress hormones while boosting immune function, easing anxiety, lowering blood pressure and cholesterol, and enhancing mood. As you chant, sound vibrations impart an invisible aura of powerful positive energy in the space around and outward from you wherever the energy flows.

Mantras may be ritually chanted for healing, rejuvenation, invigoration, and spiritual advancement. Chanting exalts your positive thoughts and feelings and empowers you to draw into your orbit helpful people, new opportunities, and desirable situations according to the ancient spiritual law of attraction. Most importantly, the positivity that arises from your chanting is a factor in robust health, happiness, and longevity. If you don't know a mantra, chant the ancient Sanskrit mother of all mantras, Om (pronounced "Aum"). This pure primordial sound is often used to open and close spiritually charged prayers and scriptures. Roll chanting beads through your fingers as you form the sounds. Also known as prayer beads, chanting beads help you keep track of the number of times you recite a chant or do a cycle of breaths in meditation. Chanting is all about the sound vibration that you feel resonating during the chanting, and that you can use to infuse your life with positive energy.

RITUAL 4.
SNIFF A MEMORY

USE SCENT TO SHIFT INTO A HEALTHIER, HAPPIER MOOD

The connection between scent and memory begins in the womb and develops as you grow. Your nose learns to detect thousands of scents and to associate certain odors with special memories. Two olfactory receptors in your nasal passages carry odors to the limbic system (the ancient, primitive part of the brain believed to be the seat of emotion). You may respond emotionally to a scent even before you can recognize and name it.

Odors that bring up pleasant memories lift your mood, which contributes to good health, enhances creativity, and boosts problem-solving abilities.

Keep at the ready a vial of essential oil that you associate with a pleasant personal memory or choose lemon (for cheerfulness), lavender (for stress-relieving clarity), and rosemary (for energy). On a facecloth folded in half and then half again, place a drop or two on the top fold.

1. Close your eyes.
2. Hold the scented cloth under your nose.
3. Allow a fond memory to rise in your thoughts.
4. Inhale gently to the count of four.
5. Hold to the count of four.
6. Exhale to the count of eight and repeat at least three times.

Use this ritual anytime you feel the need to return to a happier emotional state.

RITUAL 5.
USE BIJA SEED SOUNDS

RESTORE BALANCE TO
YOUR SEVEN CHAKRAS

The ancient Vedic tradition teaches that certain sound vibrations have the power to stimulate transformational growth and foster robust health. These particular sounds are known as *bija* (or single-syllable sounds) and are associated with your seven main chakras. Chakras are centers along the spine where energy is intensely focused. These chakra locations (situated from the base of the spine to the top of your head) receive and radiate the energy throughout your mind-body system. When chakra energy is impeded or disrupted, mental and physical health can be adversely affected. Conversely, when the chakras are aligned and in good balance, you'll notice a sharpened mental acuity, robust creativity, and expansion of consciousness.

Chant the sound for each chakra six to ten times while feeling the sound vibrate at the back of your throat and through your lips.

1. Muladhara (root chakra)—Lam
2. Svadhisthana (navel chakra)—Vam
3. Manipura (solar plexus chakra)—Ram
4. Anahata (heart chakra)—Yam
5. Vishuddha (throat chakra)—Ham
6. Ajna (third-eye chakra)—Om
7. Sahasrara (crown chakra)—Om

Take your chakra tune-up one step further; locate and listen to a chakra tune-up sequence on *YouTube* or on an app that you download from iTunes. Listen, hum, and feel that vibe tune up.

RITUAL 6.
RELISH THE RAINBOW

DINE ON TASTY, COLORFUL FOODS

Whether you call the newest healthy food craze a Buddha bowl, hippie bowl, rainbow bowl, or bowl of ancient grains and veggies, it's guaranteed to deliver plenty of balanced nutrition to keep your body and brain healthy. For a lunchtime ritual, create a vitamin- and mineral-packed nourishing bowl of rainbow-colored foods. Include fresh or cooked veggies, fruit, protein, and fat but limit the carbohydrates. Follow these simple steps.

1. Establish a base of colorful, freshly washed leafy greens such as kale, spinach, and a variety of lettuces in a midsized bowl.
2. Add raw veggies such as green broccoli, yellow sweet corn, sliced purplish beets, red onion, orange carrots, beige mushrooms, and white swords of jicama, or cooked vegetables such as green lentils and others of various colors and sizes.
3. Drop in protein-rich ingredients (grilled meat, egg, or tofu).
4. Add a source of healthy fat (fish, avocado, nuts).
5. Sprinkle nuts, seeds, or berries over the top, and toss together if you desire to mix the ingredients.

Practice Buddhist mindfulness. Tune out all distracting thoughts and focus your whole body-mind awareness on what you are experiencing in a single moment. Remain fully absorbed in this practice as you enjoy, for example, a carrot, a string bean, or an apple slice. Contemplate the Source of that morsel and feel gratitude for the good it does your body.

RITUAL 7.
SPRINKLE IN TURMERIC

GAIN POTENT HEALTH BENEFITS
FROM THIS SACRED SPICE

Ensure you have a container of turmeric in your spice carousel if you want a powerful ingredient for maintaining good health and treating a host of maladies. Add this yellow spice that yogis associate with the solar plexus chakra to your ancient grains, rice, roasted potatoes, grilled squash, soups, curries, and beverages such as green juices and teas.

According to Siddha medicine, the ancient healing tradition of the Southeast Asia Tamil culture, a healthy soul must have a healthy body. Siddha science views turmeric as a potent medicine. In Ayurveda (Indian traditional medicine), turmeric is believed to help sufferers of arthritis, heartburn, high cholesterol, and liver ailments. Modern science has demonstrated turmeric's anti-inflammatory, antiviral, antifungal, and antioxidant properties due to turmeric's active ingredient curcumin and possible other turmeric components. Although research is ongoing, a different compound in turmeric known as ar-turmerone has been found to stimulate stem cell repair in the brain, and studies suggest the spice protects against Alzheimer's.

After a ritual meditation and oblation, make yourself a cup of ginger or green tea by steeping the tea with almond milk and a pinch of turmeric. Add honey to sweeten. After offering your libation to the Universe, relax and enjoy your drink with the knowledge that it doesn't just taste delicious; it's good for your body and soul.

RITUAL 8.
EAT FOR EYE HEALTH

CHOMP ON CARROTS AND POWERHOUSE GREENS

Eyes are your organ of sight, giving you the ability to perceive shapes, distances, colors, and motions. Your vision is critical to almost everything you do. To keep it healthy, eat your carrots, spinach, and kale. Carrots contain beta-carotene, a type of vitamin A that benefits the retina and other parts of the eye. Foods that are packed with nutrients for healthy eyes can be found among the leafy greens. Spinach and kale, for example, are high in the powerful antioxidants of lutein and zeaxanthin and are excellent for counteracting eye tissue exposure to sunlight, pollution, and cigarette smoke. To stave off age-related vision loss, cataracts, and macular degeneration, choose vegetables and fruits that contain high amounts of lutein and zeaxanthin as well as vitamins C and E and omega-3 fatty acids.

Good sources of vitamin C include strawberries, papaya, oranges, grapefruit, Brussels sprouts, and green peppers. To keep eye tissue strong and healthy, choose foods that are high in vitamin E such as almonds, pecans, sunflower seeds, and wheat germ. Make it your daily ritual to include these foods in your Buddha bowl or incorporate them into a smoothie. Offer a prayer before indulging your taste buds and afterward give thanks.

RITUAL 9.
REENERGIZE YOUR EYES

USE THE HEELS OF YOUR
HANDS TO WARM THEM

If you experience eye fatigue after hours of staring at a computer screen, studying for tests, watching an event, perusing documents, or gazing at an electronic device, you're not alone. Approximately 90 percent of all computer users whose work involves staring at a computer monitor for three hours or more during the day may suffer from one or more of the common symptoms of tired eyes. These include light sensitivity, focusing difficulty, dry eyes, droopy lids, and headaches. For a quick eye refresher, place chilled cucumber slices, a bag of frozen peas, or a washcloth saturated with cold water or milk over your closed lids. Alternatively, try this simple eye yoga technique.

1. Relax in a chair and close your eyes.
2. Take five deep breaths in and out.
3. Rub your palms together briskly to generate heat.
4. Place your palms on your closed eyes and feel the heat warming the tissues around the eyelids.
5. Relax deeply into the darkness and warmth for as long as you can feel the heat.
6. Repeat the steps several more times as needed.

Your eyes will feel less weary, revitalized, and better able to focus.

RITUAL 10.
SEE SIGNS OF HEALTH ISSUES

Check Your Nails

Nails often hold clues to the state of your health. Healthy nails are strong, smooth, and pink. Pale nails can be a sign of anemia, malnutrition, liver disease, and even heart failure. White nails and jaundiced fingers signal issues with liver health. Yellow, thickening nails are a common sign of fungal infection and in rare instances might be indicating lung or thyroid disease or diabetes. Unpainted natural nails that show a bluish tint reveal a lack of oxygen, which could be due to a lung or heart ailment. Inflammatory arthritis can show up in the early stages in nails with ridges or ripples. Take a moment during your shower or bath routine to notice your nails. Groom them often or get a professional manicure.

If you enjoy doing yoga with pals, especially all those fun sequences that make you bend, twist, stretch, and work your body, get those nails in shape because everyone's going to see them. Enjoy a spa day once a month that includes a manicure and pedicure. It doesn't have to mean going to a salon, although you could. Treat yourself or do your mani-pedi with a buddy and examine your nails together.

RITUAL 11.
FIND TIME FOR ECOTHERAPY

EXPERIENCE NATURE'S HEALING MAGIC

Time in nature, sometimes referred to as *ecotherapy*, fosters well-being in body, mind, and spirit. According to a 2007 study in the United Kingdom, when participants who suffered from seasonal affective disorder (SAD) and depression went for a green or country walk, 71 percent of them felt less depressed. The healing vitality and presences in nature can alleviate stress, increase creativity, and empower you to reconnect with the ancient power of healing that nature holds. Keep a clover or flower in your pocket to remind you to return to nature. Take a walk in green space or do a weekly hike in the mountains, out on the prairie, along a river or lake, down a country road, or across a field. Ritualize your excursion by practicing mindfulness. Take time to breathe fresh air. Run your fingers in splashing water from a waterfall or trace the boundary of a warm ancient stone.

RITUAL 12.
SAVOR BETTER SLEEP

IMPROVE HEART HEALTH THROUGH YOGA NIDRA

You may need six to nine hours of good sleep nightly, but are you getting it? Clearing away the chaos of the day isn't always easy. Sometimes just getting to sleep proves difficult. But sleep is how the body and brain heal and cells renew. Yoga nidra ("yogic sleep") involves deep conscious relaxation to release muscle tension and emotions trapped in your subconscious after a hectic day. Do yoga nidra as your body hits those cool cotton sheets. Deep, restorative sleep will soon engulf you.

1. Lie in the Corpse Pose (Savasana).
2. Focus your attention on the right foot and ankle.
3. Move your attention slowly up the whole limb. Relax it.
4. Repeat the process for the left lower limb.
5. Mentally check in with your pelvis, tummy, and torso.
6. Shift your attention to your right shoulder and guide your attention along the arm down to your hand and fingers. Feel the whole limb relax.
7. Repeat step 6 for the left shoulder, arm, and hand.
8. Breathe in, breathe out with an awareness of all the sensations in your body.
9. Turn onto your right side, where left nostril breathing cools your body (lying on your right side means the left nostril is higher than the right and air flows easily and without restriction through the left). Relax.
10. Roll onto your back. Deepen the relaxation until you cross the threshold into restorative sleep.

RITUAL 13.
ADOPT LAGOM

A Balanced Approach
to Good Health

The new Scandinavian trend in wellness is encapsulated in a single word, *lagom*—"just the right amount." Apply this practical philosophy of balance, moderation, and frugality to your lifestyle choices that impact health, such as eating, drinking, exercising, sleeping, and de-stressing. The idiomatic expression that "less is more" finds resonance in lagom because overindulging can have negative consequences on health. Lifestyle choices can adversely or positively affect a person's health. With lagom as your guiding principle—neither too excessive nor too sparse, your lifestyle choices are based on balance, wisdom, and simplicity. Incorporate rituals of lagom into your life by regularly cleaning your supplement, medicine, and food cabinets; keep the right amount of what you need and toss or recycle inessential, packaged, or old items. Eat higher quality fresh foods in smaller quantities and release unhealthy habits such as overconsumption of sugar and salt. Keep well hydrated with enough daily water, and get the right amount of sleep. Exercise, but don't overdo it.

Like the Swedes, from whom the term *lagom* comes, use lagom as a blueprint for a way of living and fostering your best health now. Enjoy a cup of warm milk, tea, or coffee without an abundance of additives that make a beverage taste like a sweet dessert and let lagom liberate you with the idea that "just enough" is just right. Let the milk or coffee taste linger on your tongue.

RITUAL 14.
DO A RITUAL SCRAPE

Maintain Oral Health

In the ancient practice of Ayurveda, ritual scraping of the tongue each morning is paramount to keeping the oral cavity free of bacteria and maintaining excellent oral health. Scraping removes any coating or residue built up overnight as a result of gastrointestinal imbalances or improper digestion. Scraping just might enhance your ability to taste food even as it rids your mouth of any unpleasant odors and reduces the chances for bacteria to breed on the keratin (dead cells that form a thin callus on the tongue). They are typically present and in check. Overabundance produces a coated tongue. The *Charaka Samhita*, the Sanskrit text on the Ayurvedic system of medicine, recommends that the scraping instrument should be curved so as not to injure the tongue and made from metals that include gold, silver, copper, tin, and brass (today, many are stainless steel).

Ayurveda practitioners can diagnose the health of your body by an examination of your tongue; they suggest that a clean tongue and oral cavity not only benefits the health of the overall body but also affects the clarity of the mind. A thickly coated tongue indicates toxicity. Make scraping part of your daily regimen of hygiene. Gently scrape your tongue from the back to the front seven or more times and then brush and floss for a mouthful of refreshing clean. Kiss your fingers and blow a kiss to the Universe for a new day of good health and a bright and creative mind.

RITUAL 15.
LACE UP OR KICK OFF
YOUR SHOES AND GET GOING

EXERCISE FOR BETTER
HEALTH AND SEX

When you've had a long, stressful day at work and are facing an evening of chores such as preparing dinner, doing laundry, and helping the kids with homework, you might not feel like exercising. However, exercise is just what you need. Thirty minutes of walking, working out in a gym, or doing tai chi can stimulate chemicals in your brain to help you feel reinvigorated, relaxed, and happier. If you hate the idea of exercising alone, do your workout earlier in the day. Join a dance troupe or a swim or soccer team. Exercise improves your energy, stamina, sex life, cardiovascular health, and weight loss while also reducing your risk for chronic diseases such as depression, type 2 diabetes, arthritis, certain cancers, and metabolic syndrome.

Aim for thirty minutes of daily exercise five days each week. As your stamina improves, lengthen your workout period. You'll discover it boosts your thinking power, confidence, self-esteem, and bone health. Sit quietly after exercise and feel your pulse pounding, your heart beating, and your lungs rhythmically inhaling and exhaling. Feel gratitude and give thanks for the energy that supports your healthy body as well as the Universe.

RITUAL 16.
ENJOY PRENATAL YOGA

Discover Benefits
of Simple Asanas

Pregnancy is both an exciting time and one fraught with many vagaries. To stay relaxed, centered, and flexible as you experience a host of bodily changes that accompany pregnancy, consider joining a women-only prenatal yoga class. You will change as your baby grows inside you. Pregnancy often triggers heightened sensitivity in taste and smell. You may also experience moments of irrationality or forgetfulness. It is also not unusual to have worry or fear. Prenatal yoga practices can help you find your way to serenity and peace. Certain yoga stretches and poses can alleviate some of the pain associated with pregnancy—the main culprits being sciatica and low back pain.

Doing a regular hatha yoga practice will benefit you and your unborn baby, especially during the first trimester. The prevailing wisdom is to avoid raising your core body temperature to protect the developing infant. Of course, you'll want to check with your health-care provider before starting any new exercise regimen, especially during pregnancy. Join a weekly class with other pregnant women to do poses such as the cat stretch, simple deep breathing pranayama, and meditation. These three rituals with an emphasis on the mind-body connection can give you relief from cramping at the delivery time, since your ability to relax and breathe your way through cramps can ease the birthing process.

RITUAL 17.
KEEP YOUR GUT HEALTHY

EAT FERMENTED TO FOSTER
GOOD GUT HEALTH

Your health depends on what you eat. The foods you consume dictate how healthy your gut will be. That, in turn, affects everything about your body from skin appearance to energy level, weight, mental clarity, and immunity to illness. Every human body is filled with bacteria, fungi, and viruses—what science calls our individual microbiome, which can become unbalanced through bad diet, lack of exercise, and exposure to toxins in the environment. New research suggests it might be possible to reshape the microbiome with a daily regimen that involves eating a diet of highly nutritious diversified foods (including fermented) and doing exercise, which strengthens your immune system, reduces inflammation, and improves overall health. The secret to fantastic gut health is an internal environment that supports diverse intestinal bacteria.

Fermented foods (probiotics) are abundant with active bacteria such as *Lactobacillus* and *Bifidobacterium* as well as yeasts. These gut foods promote a healthy microbiome that in turn affects brain, organ, and skin health. If you want radiant skin, mental clarity, and youthful energy, you must safeguard your gut's health. Eat a daily serving of probiotic (such as yogurt, kefir, sauerkraut, or kimchi) and bless that tangy taste as a symbol of your healthful intentions.

RITUAL 18.
TRY ACUPUNCTURE AS PREVENTATIVE THERAPY

IMPROVE ENERGY FLOW

In traditional Chinese medicine, acupuncture is an ancient healing and health modality (that is, mode of practice to diagnose and treat) used to diagnose and resolve imbalances that cause distress and disease. The trained practitioner inserts long, thin, fine needles shallowly into points along specific pathways (acupressure points) of your body to detect imbalances in the flow of energy (known as qi or chi) along distinct channels of the body. Imbalances are believed to account for a host of ailments and conditions including low back pain, arthritis, digestive issues, fibromyalgia, headaches, and post-traumatic stress. Many practitioners suggest that acupuncture might be able to prevent stress, improve immunity, and boost energy. Research suggests that during acupuncture, an increase in the enzyme adenosine that occurs naturally in all cells of the body and also the release of endorphins (the brain's pain-killing chemicals) are responsible for easing pain.

Whether you have an aching back, sports injury, or low energy, an acupuncture treatment might help. Check with your physician first and then find a licensed acupuncturist. Schedule a regular visit (monthly or more often) for an energy tune-up with a little needle magic in the hands of a qualified traditional Chinese medicine practitioner.

RITUAL 19.
SAVOR SUBLIME GREEN TEA

RITUALIZE BEVERAGE BREAKS WITH A QUIET MIND

Are you one of the millions of workers who are addicted to coffee on the way to work—you know, that cupful of supersweet, no whip, skimmed milk and coffee concoction or the one with an extra drizzle of flavor on top that you get in the drive-through for a pre-work pick-me-up? Maybe it's time to create a new ritual that focuses on a less frenetic way of getting off to an energetic start. Loaded with polyphenols (antioxidants) and flavonoids (catechins) believed to prevent cell damage, green tea also boosts energy. Choose a place for your tea break where you can enter into a quiet mindfulness and focus on the nuances of flavor. Select a lovely antique cup or mug or tea bowl for your teatime ritual. For powdered green tea, you'll need to fill your tea ball (small metal mesh basket on a chain) and steep the tea in warm, not boiling, water. Try these teas for starters.

- Sencha—traditional Japanese green tea
- Genmaicha—green tea with roasted brown puffed rice
- Gyokuro—a variety of green tea grown in the shade

Green tea lowers cholesterol and increases blood flow, which is good for the heart and blocks plaque formations linked to Alzheimer's disease.

RITUAL 20.
PRACTICE QI GONG OR TAI CHI

Improve Circulation, Balance, and Alignment

Qi gong (pronounced "chee gong") and tai chi chuan are martial arts routines that emphasize slow, deliberate, meditative movements that build balance and muscle strength and control. You use your back and core muscles as well as arms and legs in sequences of movement as one position flows smoothly into the next. Some call these forms of exercise "meditation in motion." To be done correctly the moves require your full attention, but both qi gong and tai chi can accommodate any level of fitness; you can do them if you're pregnant or older. The low-impact, slow-motion exercises strengthen your core and improve flexibility. With the Yang style—the most popular—you'll concentrate on circular motions and deep breath patterns. Studies have shown these practices lower blood pressure and cholesterol, and reduce risks associated with cardiac disease.

After taking a class or following along with a DVD, make it a ritual practice to don loose clothing, center your thoughts, and do your qi gong or tai chi for an hour each day. If you know most of the moves, put in a CD of traditional Chinese meditative music to create a relaxing and appropriate atmosphere for your practice.

SEQUENCES

Healthy Wake-Up
- Deep breathe, counting the cycles of breaths.
- Recite a mantra to invoke powerful positive energy.
- Warm your muscles and improve circulation through gentle stretching.

Healthy Meal
- Eat a Buddha bowl of rainbow colored foods.
- Add turmeric and other healthy herbs and spices.
- Refresh with a cup of delicious green tea.

Healthy Vision
- Nourish your vision with foods for the eyes.
- Nurture tired eyes with a warm massage.
- Rest your eyes through deep and relaxing yoga nidra.

Life-Affirming Recharge
- Nourish body-mind-spirit with ecotherapy in the great outdoors.
- Loosen up with qi gong or tai chi.
- Spend time in nature.
- Try acupuncture.

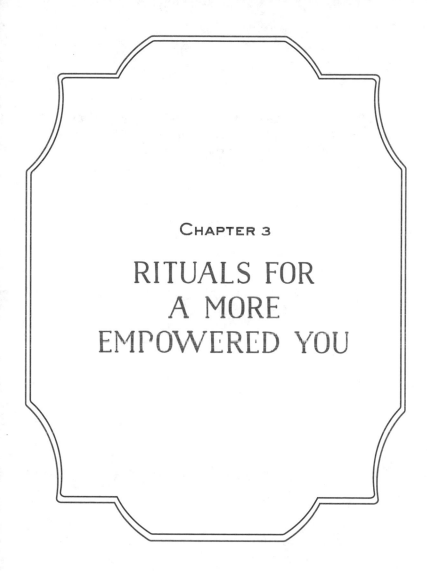

CHAPTER 3

RITUALS FOR
A MORE
EMPOWERED YOU

Within you is a powerful energy—it is your essential nature or pure consciousness; it's what you use to design and express the life you are living.

Use the words "I am" as your secret key to unlock the power to create your life and manifest what your ego wants. Whether your thoughts focus on the positive or the negative, they are attracting into your orbit what you think about most. You can easily see why you wouldn't want to emphasize what you don't want and instead focus on what you deeply desire. Ancient wisdom emphasized the importance of spending time in nature, solitude, and meditation in order to know your true Self (or soul). When you make the "I am" declaration so often that you believe it and feel a deep emotional connection with that truth and have the intention to manifest your desire, a change happens in the energy matrix. Your intention (expressed through your thoughts, emotion, rituals such as affirmations, and gratitude) sets up a magnetic attraction to draw to you what you want, whether from your ego or your true Self.

RITUAL 21.
DISCOVER YOUR INNER LIGHT

Nourish Your Skin

You feel more empowered when you look and feel great. Real and lasting beauty comes from emotional maturity, wisdom, spiritual presence, adaptability, and resilience—these originate in your heart. That doesn't mean you should ignore the care and feeding of your body's largest organ—your skin, which is what others see first. Your outer appearance reflects the inner you. Care for your body—meditate to feel peace and de-stress, deep breathe to bring more oxygen to your cells, get enough sleep, eat nutritious foods, drink lots of water, and limit your skin's exposure to the sun, environmental pollution, and toxic substances. Find and use an all-natural anti-aging face cream or make your own with rich emollients such as almond oil, vitamin E oil, coconut oil, beeswax, and shea butter. A few drops of essential oil for fragrance is optional.

- If you want luminous beauty that glows throughout your lifetime, look inside yourself. Frequent contact with your inner luminosity will manifest externally as well, in serenity and grace.
- Care for your skin daily. Wash your face, gently dry, and apply an all-natural, nourishing emollient on your skin for a healthy glow that reflects the inner you throughout a lifetime.
- Bust stress by eliminating stressors where possible; sink deeply into moments of tranquility.

RITUAL 22.
BOOK AN AYURVEDIC MASSAGE

RELEASE AND EMBRACE

In Sanskrit, Ayurveda means "life-knowledge" and is often defined as an ancient healing system that focuses on the balance of a person's whole being or body-mind-spirit. To enter into your fullness of being and to feel empowered, you might need to let go of more than tension. Ayurvedic massage addresses the needs and issues of your whole being—physical, mental, and emotional. The ancient practice helps you unlock your greatness by detoxifying and cleansing the body, reducing stress, strengthening the nervous system, promoting excellent circulation, nourishing your skin, and boosting your immune system. As your Ayurvedic massage therapist navigates his or her way through the knots you have in your body, relax into your inner world where you recognize and release what comes up emotionally and embrace new ideas that are gifts from your imagination or intellect.

Massage can be a powerful tool for releasing negativity (emotional, mental, and physical) that hurts and holds you back. Before your massage begins, the Ayurvedic massage therapist may recite a mantra. This is the perfect time for you to mentally recite your mantra for empowerment before his or her hands touch your body: "I let go of all that needs to be released and open myself to all that comes to bless me for my highest good."

RITUAL 23.
FIND YOUR INNER POWER

ASSERT YOURSELF

Your personal power doesn't have much to do with your unappreciative boss, a lack of recognition by your spouse for how hard you work, or an economy that makes it difficult to rise on the socioeconomic ladder. These are all external factors that you can't control. That doesn't mean giving in to powerlessness and hopelessness. There are things you can do. Don't give your power away to others. If you are stuck, find an escape route. Recognize that spark of the divine within you. Love and revere who you are. A daily ritual of therapeutic self-empowerment can help. Many southwestern Native American tribes carve images such as the bear to gain power over problems. They believe a mystical power is released once the image has been created. Let the image of a bear guide you back to your sense of power.

Hold the picture or statue of a bear in the palm of your right hand. Cup your left palm over your right. Close your eyes and mentally affirm: "I am the architect of my life. My power comes from the center of my being where it links to the Source of all that exists, seen or unseen. I call upon this invincible power, knowing it never fails, I give thanks for all the gifts it brings to me."

RITUAL 24.
CULTIVATE YOUR
INNER MAGNIFICENCE

PRACTICE DEEP BREATHING

If you aren't living your best life now, what's holding you back? An honest exploration of that question can help you decide how to reconfigure your life from where you are. Many tools are available today to transform the life you have into the one you want—past stagnation, fear, and fear of failure or criticism. Remember that your life's journey is what matters, not the destination. How will you breathe forth an inspired life and manifest your great gifts—qualities, virtues, talents, and abilities—in the world? Begin by deep breathing.

Sit with a straight spine, palms open on your thighs. Inhale to the count of four and exhale to the count of eight. On each inhalation, ask yourself: what do I love doing so much that it makes my spirit lighter, my heart happier, and my whole being feel rapture at the thought of doing it? Exhale and sit in silence as the answer comes.

RITUAL 25.
GIVE THE GIFT OF LIFE

Choose to Give Blood to Another

Giving blood is an act of human kindness. You will be sharing the most intimate gift you have (that which sustains your life) to save the life of another. For a multitude of reasons, an estimated one in three of us will need to receive a blood donation sometime during our lifetime. Giving blood doesn't hurt—the needle feels similar to a sharp pinch of your fleshy underarm. Your plasma is replaced in about twenty four hours; red blood cells will take four to six weeks. You won't be doing it for the juice and cookie given to you afterward; you'll be doing it as an act of empowerment to help another human being who hasn't asked, who doesn't know you, and whom you'll probably never meet.

If you are healthy and can give the gift of life, consider making a ritual donation every eight weeks, preceded by a silent mental attunement to a higher power, a healthy meal, and water.

1. Appeal: "May the blood that sustains my life preserve the life of him or her who will receive this gift. Blessings be upon both of us. Om, shanti (peace), Amen."
2. Eat nutritious meals always, but especially before and also after donating.
3. Drink sixteen ounces of water before and after giving.

RITUAL 26.
CULTIVATE A SENSE OF PURPOSE

GET ON COURSE
WITH YOUR PASSION

If you are someone who feels you are not on purpose with your life, do something about it. Living on purpose gives your life meaning. Some people walk through their lives half asleep, dreaming of the past, worrying about the future, missing the opportunities in each moment to be alert and aware and in tune with what they believe is their destiny. When you wake up to your life and follow your passion, you feel intensely alive. That sense of vitality translates to better health and well-being. Your self-esteem is strengthened. You have increased resiliency in the face of challenges and difficulties.

Create a space in your home or workplace where you can retreat from the world. Go there often to sit—tailbone to floor pillow, yoga mat, or chair seat—in an unhurried silence.

- Let tranquility wash over you.
- Listen deeply to inner guidance (intuitive thoughts relayed from your Higher Self).
- Meditate on whatever it is you are meant to do and be.
- Spend time in your space to creatively imagine your purposeful life. Jot down in a journal what comes up for you from your well of inner wisdom. Soon you'll have a sense of purpose and direction.

RITUAL 27.
DEVELOP DEEP SELF-LOVE

INCREASE YOUR PASSION AND CREATIVITY

During infancy and early childhood, a person must receive love and emotional connections if he or she is to feel worthy and lovable as an adult. When those basic needs aren't met, the adult struggles with relationship and abandonment issues. See your body, mind, and spirit as unique and worthy of self love. Loving yourself, you are then able to share your love with others. This self-care isn't narcissism but rather a cultivation of a tender loving-kindness to achieve healthy selfhood. When you tune into the guidance available to you within the secret places of your soul and feel valued, you become empowered to foster meaningful connections with others. This empowerment, in turn, helps your passion and creativity to thrive.

Begin writing daily in a journal or a SMASH book that celebrates your life. In it, write a daily positive affirmation to yourself. Keep expressions simple; for example, "My body is healthy," or "My heart is peaceful and loving," or "My mind is imaginative." Or, "I am wise." Paste or draw images and symbols from your meditation and dreams. Jot down any inner guidance. See your mind as wildly creative; see your body as an old friend that has brought you from infancy to adulthood, ever loyal and faithful and never abandoning you.

RITUAL 28.
PERMEATE A SHAWL WITH PRANA

CONCENTRATE YOUR
SPIRITUAL ENERGIES

Cloths or shawls that have been consecrated have a long tradition as ritual tools of healing. Also used to symbolize spiritual power and faith, a consecrated shawl can be energized (when you wrap it around you during meditation) with the life-force energy of prana, the same powerful energy filling the Universe.

Dip your finger into fragrant oil and trace a small sacred symbol on a tiny corner of your shawl. Wrap it around your shoulders whenever you sit for meditation. The shawl provides a light layer of warmth, desirable when your activity ceases, your thoughts turn inward, and your body cools down. The act of placing a consecrated shawl around your shoulders can connect you with the inner strength of your soul. The shawl imparts a sense of holy embrace as you prepare to loosen the grip of worldly concerns to contact the most magnificent part of you—your inner Self.

RITUAL 29.
CREATE YOUR NARRATIVE

BE CREATIVE AND COURAGEOUS

Steve Jobs famously noted, "Your time is limited so don't waste it living someone else's life." That touches a nerve in all who feel that their hopes and dreams were hijacked somewhere along the way. The unfolding of your life is under your control. *You* get to decide whether or not to let someone else's voice drown out your own and when or if to follow someone else's plans or follow your heart and intuition to where and how you want to go. You came here to be someone. Staying true to yourself means you've got an anchor to stay connected to what's genuine and real. It means you possess the courage to be vulnerable and imperfect but to show up for your life anyway. Forget who you think you are supposed to be and embrace who you truly are.

Light a pink candle (if you want, hold a gemstone) and affirm: "I am capable, creative, and courageous. Every day in every way, I live my best life guided by my heart, intuition, and good judgment."

RITUAL 30.
BE COURAGEOUS

FIND WAYS TO BE RESILIENT WHEN ADVERSITY STRIKES

Call it bad karma or an unfortunate happening at an inopportune time, but adversity shows up sooner or later in every life. You might have heard the sayings "Pull yourself up by your bootstraps" and "Just work smarter, not harder." When summoning the courage to deal with adversity feels burdensome, and the situation too complicated to be easily resolved, try a simple ritual for personal protection and empowerment. The Sri Yantra is a sacred, mystical symbol in Hinduism in the form of a geometric diagram featuring nine interlocking triangles. Meditation on the sacred geometry of Sri Yantra protects from harmful forces and aids in attracting wealth, power, and success.

For new ideas and structures to arise, old ones often must give way. Destruction or adversity happening in real time requires all the courage you can muster. Tap the power of Shiva to renew. Eastern traditions believe that Shiva's cosmic dance of destruction generates renewal. Apply a dot of sandalwood paste on the statue of Shiva's forehead and yours. Sit in the cross-legged meditative pose of Shiva, find your center, and dive deeply into the silence while letting go of everything you've been trying to hang on to so renewal and rebirth can begin.

RITUAL 31.
FULFILL A DREAM

TAKE RESPONSIBILITY FOR MAKING A DREAM COME TRUE

When you put your dreams on hold to help someone else attain his or hers, your selfless action is praiseworthy. However, if you wait too long to chase your cherished visions, conditions for achieving them may change, your priorities might shift, or you may abandon all hope of ever attaining your dreams. You get married, have children, and realize that you are too busy meeting the demands of daily life head-on. Alternatively, perhaps you still secretly nurture the idea of achieving your cherished dream and just thinking about it fills you with excitement, energy, and a sense of adventure. A ritual might help jump-start it again. Begin this process by writing your dream on a card in felt tip marker. Holding it in your palms, do the following.

1. Mentally banish fear; release limited and dis-beliefs.
2. Kindle feelings of self-worth for your desire to have that dream.
3. Ask the Universe for what you want; use precise language.
4. Open yourself to opportunities that make achieving your dream possible.
5. Let go and trust that your dream has moved from a state of improbable to certain attainment.

RITUAL 32.
SET BOUNDARIES

PRACTICE SAYING "NO"

When you're overworked, stressed out, and energy depleted, how do you find time to feel empowered or to do anything creative to show your inner greatness? You learn to set boundaries so that you can stop doing something to open an hour or two to pursue personal interests. That might mean that you have to occasionally say no to family, friends, even your boss. You don't have to abandon civility and good manners. In situations where a simple "no" won't do and you can't think of a nice way to firmly decline or tell someone that you'll pass this time on taking on anything new, then practice a short sentence that will communicate the same thing, such as "It's not possible."

Whenever someone presumes to prevail on you to do more work, volunteer for yet another job or committee, or ask for favors that sap your energy and time, say, "It's just not possible." The more you repeat this, the easier it is to speak it with authority and sincerity.

RITUAL 33.
CULTIVATE YOUR UNIQUENESS

EMBRACE THE INNER QUALITIES OF SELF-IMAGE

Your values, beliefs, feelings, and opinions—what you bring out into the world of your inner being rather than what the world brings you—partly defines you. When you spend time in the solitude, it becomes easier to emphasize a spiritual image over a physical one. You can let go of a professional or personal self-image that depends on the affiliations and groups you belong to or labels others put on you. Become more aware of your inner magnificence by doing the following.

1. Be courageous and confident
2. Express your uniqueness through creative ideas
3. Listen to the voice of your soul (intuition)
4. Speak your truth
5. Love your journey more than any destination along the way

Use a diffuser with rosemary-scented oil to permeate an area where you can sit and detect the odor. As your brain brightens with clarity and energy, meditate on your unique inner attributes, talents, traits, wisdom, and gifts of the spirit and how you might use them for your good and that of others.

RITUAL 34.
FIRE UP YOUR AUTHENTIC VOICE

Speak Your Truth

If someone from the past has caused you to doubt the validity of your worth in the world and silenced your voice, find ways to reemerge, gain confidence, and speak out. In the greater Universe we may be tiny specks, but in this world you are just as important as every other person, likely with many of the same insecurities, self-doubt, emotional pain, and the false sense of not belonging. Although wounds and the bullies who inflict them are not trivial, it is possible to move from where you are. To empower your authentic voice, join a book club, community forum, or social group where disseminating ideas and expressing personal opinions are encouraged. Work with a therapist or coach.

Your throat energy center (Vishuddha chakra) balances and amplifies the power of self-expression. The chakra is associated with the color blue.

- Wash a blue lapis lazuli chakra stone in a mild saltwater solution and let it dry in the sun (to absorb solar energy).
- Lie in the Corpse Pose (flat on your back, palms up at your side) and place the stone over the center of your throat.
- Meditate on your inner divine nature and psychic gifts of the spirit.

RITUAL 35.
AWAKEN YOUR POWERFUL FEMININE

Invoke Your Maternal Instincts

In matriarchal societies in southwest China, northeastern India, and on an island west of New Guinea, women guided by their maternal principles and instincts wield great power and lead others. They make important decisions that affect the survival and well-being of their people.

They use their female perspective of mothering to foster the greatest good for themselves and benefit their families and communities. Similarly, you can access your feminine energy to make important or difficult decisions when it involves others. Contemplate your decision from a mother's perspective as leaders do in matriarchal societies, taking into account the welfare of all the people your decision will affect.

Use a triangle-shaped pendulum on a chain with a bead at the opposite end to call forth the female energy. The triangle, circle, and spiral patterns all symbolize that energy from ancient times. Sit in a chair with an arm support or next to a table where you can rest your right elbow. Clap your hands three times and then rub your palms briskly together for ten seconds. Hold your right palm parallel to the ground and slide the bead through your first and second fingers. Keep your palm straight, allowing the pendulum to dangle loosely with no obstruction. Hold your left palm facing upward under the swing point but not touching it. Invite your female energy to show its presence through the pendulum. Keep your hands still as you watch the pendulum begin to swing. The more you focus on it, the wider the circle it makes. For an answer to a yes/no question, mentally reaffirm that the pendulum will swing clockwise for yes and counterclockwise for no. At the end of the session, wrap your pendulum and put it away. Wash your hands to cool them of energy you've drawn into them.

RITUAL 36.
ENJOY A FIVE-MINUTE RENEWAL

BREAK UP YOUR BUSY CYCLES

You eat well, exercise, and get shut-eye—at least a few hours every night—before jumping back on the proverbial treadmill. Before hectic, demanding, and tiring becomes the three-word mantra for your life, take a few minutes of each day to rest, relax, and recharge. Listen to your body; it tells you when to stop pushing. No one can stay at the top of his or her game without some much-needed downtime. Throughout the day, reset your body's batteries by reconnecting with the Source of your being. Break the busy-busy cycle of work to create breathing space. Consider setting the alarm on your cell phone to sound every few hours as your spiritual call to recharge through breath work. Place a drop of sandalwood-scented oil at the third eye (the point between the eyebrows). Sit with a straight spine, palms facing upward on your thighs.

- Inhale, softly making the sound of "So."
- Exhale, making the sound of "Ham." Do the So-Ham breathing for one minute.
- Rest your consciousness in the silence for four minutes as your thoughts gravitate toward contact with the Divine.
- Feel your life-force energy being recharged and reinvigorated.

RITUAL 37.
SURROUND YOURSELF WITH
MEANINGFUL THINGS

DEFINE YOUR WORLD

Whether your sanctuary is your home or your office, determine what pleases and nurtures you and then choose furniture, art, wall color, books, and pictures of people who inspire you. Perhaps it's a settee you found in a vintage shop that lifts your spirits. Or your grandmother's drop-leaf claw-foot table that she left you in her will with a note taped to it explaining she knew how much you always loved it. Items with meaning should find a place in the interiors where you live and work precisely because they hold special memories and significance for you. Like everything in the Universe, those well-loved pieces are permeated with subtle energy from the people who've loved you and also used and loved those pieces.

Think of a beloved relative who has passed away to whom you'd like to pay tribute. Perhaps you have an old framed photo. If not, find one you like and frame it. Light a white sage smudge stick to clear the energy in the area where the picture will hang. Admire the picture when it's hung. Offer words of welcome and ask that ancestor to bless you and your space.

RITUAL 38.
CELEBRATE YOUR FRIENDSHIPS

Love Your Loyal Network

Friends bring out the best in you; they act as your reflecting mirrors, revealing your wholesomeness and best features as well as untoward, unwholesome, or unseemly actions, which they discourage. If you have a vision but can't achieve it alone, you surround yourself with the team that can make your vision a reality. It's a concept that works well in business and also in friendships. Some life experiences are difficult and challenging to face without support—for example, a natural catastrophe, life-threatening illness, business setback, or career or personal loss. Pals who care as much about you as you respect and cherish them will accompany you on your life's journey and help you navigate the pitfalls and obstacles even as they lift and inspire you. They're loyal and will keep your confidences. They rejoice at your successes and good fortune.

Waft around some attar of rose essential oil and light a pink candle (pink and rose are colors associated with love and compassion) and then write personal notes to your closest friends, expressing heartfelt appreciation for the gifts they bring to your life.

RITUAL 39.
COMMUNE WITH THE SACRED

RITUALIZE YOUR MEALS

In antiquity, there were many types of sacred meals to be found in the great spiritual and religious traditions of the East and West. The ancient Greeks kept a fire going on their home altars and on this fire, kindled with a particular wood from a certain tree, they sometimes would toss into the flames offerings of food, flowers, incense, and wine. To them, the fire was divine. A hymn to the beneficence and protection of the fire celebrates it as eternal, ever young, and nourishing. If ever extinguished, the power and the god were extinguished too. If you crave moments of ever-deeper significance in your life, deepen your soul's connection with its Source by finding more meaningful ways to shift the most mundane daily repetitions from profane to sacred. Divide your meal ritual into three significant parts, composing a beginning, a middle, and an end.

1. Before eating, to slow down and shift your focus to the food as spiritual sustenance, thank the Universe for providing your food.
2. Push grains of rice or a forkful of what's on your plate to the side and mentally offer that portion to your Inner Source.
3. Bow your head momentarily in silent gratitude that the foods are nourishing your body, just as contact with the Source nourishes your spirit.

RITUAL 40.
ADD MENTOR TO YOUR LEGACY

GUIDE SOMEONE TO BE THEIR BEST

You don't have to be at the pinnacle of your career to mentor someone. When you draw from your life experiences and knowledge base to help others achieve their best, you feel fulfilled. Mentoring also helps you stay on top of your game. Helping someone coming up the career ladder behind you forces you to keep abreast of all that's new in your field of expertise and also to figure out the best ways to share that knowledge with a rising star. Mentoring demonstrates to colleagues and bosses that you possess the skills and temperament to guide others—assets in your marketable skills toolbox.

Each time before inviting a mentee into your office, art studio, yoga retreat room, commercial kitchen, factory floor, or other job site or workplace, make a ritual cup of tea to prepare mentally.

1. Make organic green tea (use hot—not boiling—water, as the latter produces a bitter taste) and serve it to yourself in a pretty or ceremonial cup.
2. Sip slowly as you quietly contemplate what you will cover in your coming session.
3. Jot down a few notes.
4. Wash and dry your cup and put it away.

SEQUENCES

UNLEASH WHAT HOLDS YOU BACK
- Get an Ayurvedic massage to release negative emotional energy that might be impeding your progress.
- Stay centered as paradigms shift.
- Deep breathe to move your energy and consciousness.
- Plug into a higher power.

BIRTH A NEW EMPOWERED YOU
- Make loving self-care a habit.
- Power up your passion.
- Claim your authentic voice.

WORK YOUR DREAMS
- Clarify a cherished vision.
- Start doing what you're meant to do.
- Enlist loyal friends to help you.

DEEPEN YOUR SOUL CONNECTION
- Create a sacred space.
- Turn inward to nourish your spirit.
- Think like a limitless being.

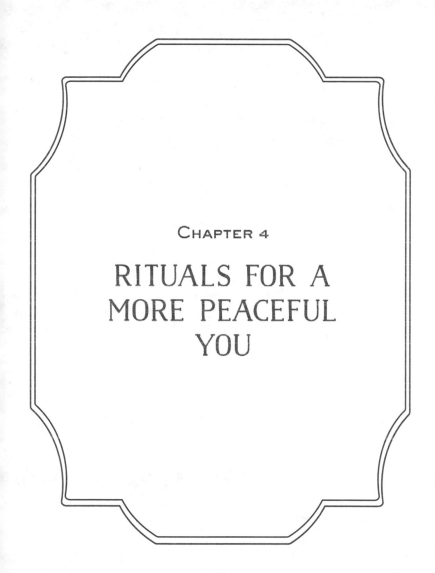

CHAPTER 4

RITUALS FOR A MORE PEACEFUL YOU

Peace is a state of tranquility and harmonious accord. When the ancient world was in upheaval due to natural and political disasters, the absence of disturbances (or, peace) would have been most welcomed by those living in such dark and stressful times. Our modern world is also plagued by conflict and threats. External turmoil might be beyond your control, but you can attain inner peace. The Hindu sacred text, Yajur Veda, counsels against fighting "against the heavenly spirit within us" and also encourages inner peace "within my own heart." The advice resonates with many of us who face the daily challenges of living in a fast-paced, seemingly stressed-out world.

You have a choice of ways to reconnect with your inner light and tranquility. Yoke pleasant and calm thoughts to a slow and quiet cycle of breath. Engage in a guided meditation using an app. Or spend a period of time in nature where your thoughts are carried aloft on the happy sounds of birdsong in the natural environs. If you have trouble returning to a peaceful equilibrium, try a ritual to guide you more deeply inward.

RITUAL 41.
REST UNDER SCENTED SATIN

FIND SERENITY WITH A LAVENDER-SCENTED EYE PILLOW

When fatigue knows no limits, and you can't find your happy spot after crawling in bed, chances are you begin to feel anxious. What if you can't fall asleep, the hours keep ticking away, and morning comes in spite of your restless night? The next time you find yourself in that negative cycle, try slipping a silk eye pillow filled with dried lavender buds over your eyes. Gentle pressure against the eyeballs is believed to lower your heart rate and stimulate the vagus nerve, which regulates heart rate and deepens relaxation. If you sleep in a room where electronic devices are charged, use a black-out mask over the scented one to ensure that your body's natural rhythm will not become distorted by artificial lights. Purchase a satin mask or sew a rectangle the width of your eyes. Leave one side open and fill the opening with dried lavender buds (purchase at a DIY fabric or hobby shop) before stitching closed and adding elastic or ties to each edge.

After your bedtime hygiene and meditation or prayers, crawl into bed and don the satin mask and the black-out mask over it. Inhale to the count of four, exhale to the count of eight until a peaceful sleep overtakes you.

RITUAL 42.
TREAT YOUR SENSE OF SMELL

Use Floral Scents to Find Peace

If you don't have a garden of herbs and the time to extract the essential oils from plants, the easiest way to access the power of flower is to have on hand a variety of essential oils. Put an essential oil (or combination) in a diffuser to waft around your environment, or simply anoint your body with a favorite scent. If you happen to enjoy making crafts such as soaps, you can add an essential oil to ease frayed nerves after a hectic day. Use a scented soap during a relaxing bath—it's another effective way to find peace and tranquility. Thank your olfactory nerve that developed while you were still in the womb for providing easy access for scents to get right to your noggin's neurotransmitters, where they can induce certain feelings, erase brain fog and restore clarity, and even heal. Perhaps the most beneficial essential oil for banishing stress, heartache, and worry is ylang-ylang because it induces a calm, relaxing effect and reduces heart rate and blood pressure even as it increases attention.

Dab ylang-ylang essential oil on the pulse points of your wrists or create a calming blend of scents by adding sweet orange, almond, and blue tansy.

RITUAL 43.
FORGIVE OLD HURTS

CREATE A SPACE FOR PEACE

The natural state of your true Self is one of joy and rapture. Holding on to anger and pain toward someone you haven't been able to forgive for a hurt inflicted in the past only agitates your mental suffering: you feel angry, sad, confused, and less positive about life. Such feelings hamper your spiritual progress and can take a toll on your health. Conversely, forgiveness can bring you a healthier attitude, lower blood pressure, less hostility, and higher self-esteem and psychological well-being. Place the value of your good health over holding on to a grudge.

Discuss your feelings with a trusted friend, listen to forgiveness tapes, or seek professional help, if necessary, but find a way to let go, forgive, and focus on the here and now. When you do, you create room in your heart and mind for peace to enter.

RITUAL 44.
SIP A POWERHOUSE ELIXIR

FEEL PEACE ENTERING THE PORES OF YOUR BEING

Saffron derives from the stigmas (red-orange threads) of the saffron crocus flower and is rich in minerals, vitamins, and antioxidants vital for good health. It also contains crocin, a water-soluble carotene associated with apoptosis (death of cancer cells) in many different human cancers, including leukemia and colon adenocarcinoma. Health specialists value turmeric for its antioxidant and anti-inflammatory powers, but it also can interfere negatively with other supplements and impede blood clotting, so check with your physician before adding this spice to your diet. While saffron and turmeric are gaining in popularity, these spices have long been known in the ancient Ayurvedic medicine tradition for their anti-inflammatory and detoxifying effects.

Combine in a blender with your favorite milk (almond or coconut) and sweeten with local organic honey and you have a potent, rejuvenating elixir for mind, body, and spirit. After a period of meditation, offer your drink to your Inner Source and then enjoy this powerhouse potion as *prasada*, which, in the Hindu tradition, is a food gift that becomes blessed through your action of offering it to the Divine. Once offered, it becomes a sacred potion to bless the devotee as he or she consumes it.

RITUAL 45.
FIND PEACE DURING UNCERTAINTY

SEE CHANGE AS GOOD

Because life is dynamic, it is unpredictable and uncertain. Some people adapt easier than others to change. When the turbulence of not knowing forces you outside your comfort zone, you might feel anxiety, distress, and fear. In meditation you can sense the steadiness underlying all uncertainty and find refuge therein. All change provides opportunities to move in new directions, gain a new perspective as you view the world through a different lens, and find unique gifts that change calls forth in you. Remember that uncertainty and mystery are transformative impermanent energies ever cycling through life.

- Sit cross-legged on your yoga mat or in a chair with your feet flat on the floor, palms cradling a small elephant carved from agate or other earth stone, ideas of stability and constancy in your thoughts. (In some cultures of the world, nothing symbolizes strength and stability like the elephant.)
- Close your eyes and visualize your root chakra (Muladhara) as a spinning red wheel at the base of your spine.
- Imagine an energy ray in a continuous loop as it flows from your root chakra to pierce deep into the earth's core and return to your chakra.
- Chant "Lam" to energize your root chakra as you meditate on peace.

RITUAL 46.
PROTECT YOURSELF IN A VISUAL BUBBLE

Don't Absorb Others' Energies

Do you avoid spending time at malls, performance venues, sports arenas, and other crowded places because being around lots of people wears you down, makes you feel stressed, or causes you to feel ill? When friends call to discuss their toxic issues, do you take on their distress? Do you absorb energies that signal fatigue, anger, pain, anxiety, or sickness in others when you pass them in the grocery store, the gas station, or large group meetings with a spiritual teacher? If you answered yes, you might be a natural empathic who is taking on the energies of other people. To protect yourself in crowds, put distance between yourself and others.

To remain peaceful, reestablish your connection to your core, close your eyes, and focus on your breath by inhaling lightness and exhaling darkness. Then visualize a bubble of white light around you as a protective shield. Mentally say the following affirmation: "I connect to the divine energy matrix that safeguards me, and ask that only positive energies enter the invisible field encircling me. I feel rooted in peace."

RITUAL 47.
PRACTICE LOVING-KINDNESS
TOWARD YOURSELF

Draw Peace with a Phrase

Think of loving-kindness as a feel-good tonic for all the little irritations during the day that disturb your peace. The easiest way to practice loving-kindness of self is through breath work and recitation of phrases that you can repeat throughout the day or incorporate in a more elaborate personal ritual. By stirring your feelings of benevolence, love, appreciation, friendliness, and gratitude toward yourself, you become empowered to radiate those feelings toward others. It is as though you are wrapping them in the warm blanket of tranquility you've created through your generosity of spirit. The first step in creating a loving-kindness ritual for peace directed toward yourself might be to come up with a phrase that you can recite mentally or aloud repeatedly throughout your day. Phrases about peace that are succinct and powerful and found in the Mass include "Peace be with you... and with your spirit...My peace I bring to you." Or you might say on the inhaled breath, "May I live in peace." On the exhaled breath, you might say, "May peace permeate my being."

Use myrrh aromatherapy in a diffuser or warmed wax burner to link your chosen phrase with a scent that will always remind you to recite those words.

RITUAL 48.
DEFLECT WHITE NOISE DAMAGE

TRY EMBODIMENT PRACTICE

Ambient sounds such as white noise, according to several studies, induces the release of cortisol, a stress hormone. An excess of that hormone can interfere with proper functioning of your brain's prefrontal cortex where planning, reasoning, and impulse controls are executed. Stressed and unable to focus, you seek peace. An excellent way of restoring peace is to engage in the Buddhist practice of mindfulness or staying focused on all the information your senses are conveying to your brain during one moment as it flows into the next and on endlessly. A relatively new technique for finding peace is what neuroscientists call "interoception" or, simply, embodiment. It is the practice of mindfulness applied to your body. From one moment to the next, you observe physical changes, but you change nothing. In the process, you gain resilience on an emotional-intellectual level and a heightened sense of well-being that brings about peace.

Sit in a chair and do belly breathing to center yourself. The technique is to place your palm on your belly, feeling your tummy expand like a balloon when you inhale, and during exhalation your belly recedes to where it was before you took in a deep breath.

RITUAL 49.
FIND PEACE THROUGH ART

DELVE DEEPLY IN ART CREATION

When you focus on an inner wellspring of trust, choose to believe in your personal power, and see all negative experiences as teaching agents, you soon discover that it's possible to have a fulfilling life and, yes, a peaceful life regardless of what is going on around you. Peace can be a choice you make at any moment. Choose an instrument of peace such as submersion in a wonder of nature or a piece of great art. Both are effective in emotional healing and as stressbusters because they shift your stressed-out attitude in a different direction—more toward amazement, wonder, awe, and a desire to explore. These emotions counter body inflammation and boost the immune system. Experience peace and healing while responding the extraordinary creations of beauty, whether the art you view is of nature and landscapes or still life, portraits, or scenes from life.

See your colored pencils, crayons, pastels, or paints and brushes as artist tools and get to work expressing a magical peace through colors and images. While creating your art, be aware of how you lose all sense of time.

RITUAL 50.
TOUCH PEACE
THROUGHOUT YOUR DAY

PUSH NEGATIVITY AWAY

External events can careen toward you out of the blue and disrupt your calm equilibrium. You feel off balance, impatient, and maybe angry because someone wants something from you immediately or you are worried about a friend or project in jeopardy. Perhaps a partner wants to redefine your relationship. When your equilibrium has been thrown off-kilter, you must decide not to give in to negative emotion; instead, consciously choose harmony. Keep a lithium quartz crystal near you or in your pocket and use it as a touchstone for feeling restored. That quartz has long been associated with calming energy, balance, and spiritual growth.

Morning: Touch the quartz and remember not to struggle; accept things as they are.

Noon: Hold the quartz and feel fully present in the peaceful flow of your life.

Four p.m.: Notice the quartz's weight and let it strengthen and intensify harmonious energies flowing around and into you.

Eight p.m.: Review your day and reject anxiety, stress, guilt, and other nonproductive emotional responses. Simply observe, choose to reject, and release all that disrupts and disturbs your mind. Claim the peace that is always available when you desire it.

RITUAL 51.
MOVE PAST PERFECTION

RELEASE CONTROL
AND INVITE PEACE

If you love to get things right every time and invest in high standards and lofty goals, falling short isn't an option. But when it happens, the voice of your inner critic might sound off loud and clear. Worse, that self-critical voice can be unrelenting, torturing you for days afterward. You might feel anger, guilt, and a whole lot of frustration at not finishing something or seeing it turn out less than perfectly. Letting go of the need for perfection might seem near impossible until you figure out how to tamp down the inner critic and move past the need to control to feel peaceful again. Once you can move past that compulsion, you open space in your being to feel harmony and balance and peace.

Light a candle scented with sweet orange, a scent favored in Europe, Arabia, and China during the tenth century to foster relaxation and warm, comforting, and peaceful feelings. Deep breathe for six breaths and then relax and focus your thoughts on things that you can do successfully rather than perfectly, which is so much easier. Repeat this process until you feel peace settle in your bones.

RITUAL 52.
RECOGNIZE YOUR UNIQUE GIFTS

TRUST YOUR SENSES
TO LEAD YOU WITHIN

You can call forth the gifts of serenity, tranquility, and peace whenever you want them through the power of your senses, of breath work, and of meditation. Emotions, often triggered by external factors beyond your control, can blow in and agitate your mind—knocking you off balance and triggering a cascade of negative thoughts. The practice of centering your mind back on your breath is a great way to deal with emotional upsets. Meditation, breath work, chanting, and yoga asanas—these are all tools available to you when you want to cultivate deep peace. When you turn inward and use your imagination, your sense of hearing allows music to usher your consciousness into the presence of your Inner Source. Your sense of smell does likewise. Touching your prayer beads will accomplish the same thing.

Download some instrumental music before you sit in meditation. Let your sense of hearing bless your meditation and carry you ever more deeply inward. When the music stops playing, feel the breeze of bliss blowing sweetly through you into the interior of your heart. Sit absorbed in silence.

RITUAL 53.
PLUNGE INTO
PEACEFUL CONSCIOUSNESS

RIDE THE WAVE

Your imagination, whether or not you realize it, is a powerful force for transformation. Modern physics describes the invisible field at the quantum level all around us as vibrations and waves of energy and information—the ultimate reality that sustains and supports the creation that we see as our world (part of a larger universe). Wisdom teachers have said that through our thoughts (which are energy), we cocreate with this field. Thoughts about your physical body, for example, can effect change at the quantum level. A change in your thinking brings about a change in the matrix. Feel peace. Feel whole, healed, and free of stress and worry, and draw that into your body-mind-spirit.

Sit in silence. Practice mindfulness as you listen for sounds in the silence. Flow with this sacred sound as it supports and carries your consciousness like a wave in a sea of rapturous peace flowing throughout the visible and invisible worlds in the infinity of space.

RITUAL 54.
EMBARK ON A PERSONAL RETREAT

FILL YOUR HEART WITH THE OPIATE OF PEACE

Time spent in solitude allows your body and mind to de-stress, rebalance, and rest. Your parasympathetic nervous system begins to relax your muscles, decrease your heart rate, and lower your blood pressure. Sleeping under the stars, you absorb the healing energies of the earth. Traveling through a mountainous landscape or swimming in a warm sea, your body attunes itself to a slow and ancient rhythm. Use your powers of observation, visualization, and imagination to take a mental snapshot of the wondrous scene around you. Long after your solitude ends, you can again summon feelings of peace and generate the same healthy benefits by reimaging your peaceful retreat.

- Dispense the scent of pine and eucalyptus (via essential oil or warm wax or candle) in an area where you can lie on your yoga mat or the carpet.
- Assume the Corpse Pose (Savasana); lie flat with head and tailbone perfectly aligned.
- Imagine you are camping in an awe-inspiring spot in nature.
- Let the cares of your life fall away and set aside all thought of your obligations (they'll still be there after you've rested).
- Let peace arise within you as you rest in the womb of eternal time.

RITUAL 55.
TAKE A NEGATIVITY BREAK

DON AN AMULET

It's a healthy practice to take a regular break from the news that is charged with negativity and stories meant to tug at your emotions (and that means the electronic delivery of it that you get through all your devices, including your smartphone). Bad news captures headlines and sells advertising. If you deal with stress and negativity during the workday, watching the news in your living room (or worse, bedroom) compounds the load your body and mind are already carrying. How you will you release the negative energy to feel protected, powerful, and peaceful?

In Thai society, monks in Buddhist temples welcome alms for necessities and money. In return, devotees are given a Gautama Buddha amulet that has been made and blessed by the monks. The wearer of the amulet (which might even contain even some ashes of old temple buildings where centuries of prayers have created positive vibrations) receives protection and blessings for good fortune. Offer a prayer of veneration and gratitude before putting on the amulet that affords peace, power, continuity, and protection. Out of respect for the Buddha, remove the amulet during bathing and do not keep it in the bedroom. When taking off the amulet, offer a prayer for its safekeeping. Locate numerous sources for amulets online or in New Age stores and import shops featuring Southeast Asian items. Alternatively, choose an amulet with a symbol or image that will remind you to return to peace whenever you wear it.

RITUAL 56.
TAKE A SENSUAL
WALK IN THE RAIN

RECAPTURE THE MAGIC
WITH POETRY

If you love taking a nature walk in the rain, noticing water drops on spiderwebs, birds disappearing into the sheltering dark canopies of trees, the sight of wet craggy outgrowths or the wind blowing cool drizzle against your face, it's probably because of what your senses are telling you. The rain's patter provides a rhythm to the scene. Your boots carry you across an ancient terrain under a shower that is taking place now in the same way it did a million years ago. There is something comforting about the continuity as you absorb the sensual experiences and steady inflow of peace into your soul. Just as the earth has a landscape of being in which you take comfort in familiar terrain, so does the inner landscape of your being.

Sit in a comfortable chair; read the sensual haiku of seventeenth-century poet Matsuo Bashō. Notice how peaceful, powerful, and evocative the poems are as they reflect landscapes in the rain or moonlight. These images come from the magical inner terrain of the poet's mind and heart. Reading and reflecting on the poetic images, notice how peace descends upon you. Disappear into it.

RITUAL 57.
GAIN PEACE OF MIND

GATHER INFORMATION USING MULTISENSORY PERCEPTION

Multisensory is a new buzzword in the wellness world. In a nutshell, you perceive your world through the five senses by tasting, touching, smelling, hearing, and seeing. These five senses link you with the outer world. Intuition is your "sixth sense," relaying information from your inner world. Taken together, your senses function as your multisensory perception of the inner and outer worlds. Intuition conveys information in different ways for different people. For example, you might sense danger through a shiver, a hunch, a warning inner voice, a frightening idea, a cold chill down your spine, or the hair standing up on your arms. As you work at recognizing what your intuition is telling you, you learn to trust it to reveal both the physical and nonphysical world. Your powers of perception lead to greater peace of mind.

Sit in a comfortable position in a quiet place where you won't be disturbed. With eyes closed, focus on your breathing sensations as you inhale through your nose and exhale through slightly opened mouth. Let your breath slow, which, in turn, slows your heart rate. Ask a short, clear, and direct question for which the answer will give you peace of mind. Feel gratitude and offer thanks to the Source of All for your intuitive power.

RITUAL 58.
GIVE YOUR SOUL EXPRESSION

EXPERIENCE THE PEACE OF SACREDNESS

Keep something beautiful in your pocket to remind you that your life and work in the world are made easier when you befriend your Soul-self (or Higher Self) that renders support and guidance from within. Entering into the presence of your Soul-self, you'll feel an intimate familiarity. The Soul has always been with you as a silent witness weaving a sacred unity out of the complex ways you rush and reach outward into the world. Choose a soul symbol—a dove (symbol of the Holy Spirit in Christianity), an amulet bearing "Om Tat Sat" (truth-consciousness-bliss, three aspects of Brahman in Hinduism), the caduceus (ida, pingala, and kundalini power), the trinity spiral (ancient goddess symbol of body-mind-spirit), or perhaps the wings of Mercury. Or, fashion your own symbol.

- Touch or gaze upon the symbol when you need to experience a lightness of being and peace.
- Breathe in. Breathe out and feel frenetic energy gathering as a dark ray leaving your aura and being transformed back into neutral energy.
- Breathe in and visualize drawing with the in-breath the positive energy of light and bliss.
- Give thanks.

RITUAL 59.
MAKE TIME FOR MEDITATION

Listen to a Meditation App

Meditation advocates quieting the mind to raise spiritual consciousness or to observe content of the mind without judging or identify-
ing with the content. Whether or not you've tried meditation, you can
begin or advance your practice through meditation applications that
can be used on e-devices. Whenever you can find fifteen or more minutes in your day, use it to meditate. Have ready your meditation app
and the e-device you'll use to play the app.

- Sit in a quiet place where you won't be interrupted.
- Light a candle and diffuse a scent that you associate with rev-
  erential peace.
- Deep breathe until your body feels calm and your mind becomes
  quiet.
- Turn on the e-device with the application and turn your focus
  inward. Your aim is to be aware of nothing inside except awareness itself.
- At the end of the session, take the blessing of light from the
  candle by waving your palms over the flame and then over your
  head. Bring your palms together in the prayer mudra (ritual
  position) at your heart and bow.

This marks the end of your session. Blow out the candle and turn
off your device.

RITUAL 60.
FIND PEACE THROUGH SELF-ACCEPTANCE

CLAIM A MORE PEACEFUL LIFE

Psychologists say that peace of mind derives from self-acceptance. Self-acceptance begins when you replace feelings of unworthiness with trust, self-respect, and value. One way to shift into a paradigm of positivity and self-worth is to hone in on what's best about you—what are your strengths? Build a support system that includes those who believe in you and sincerely desire to see you succeed. If you are holding on to pain, blame, or self-loathing for your past errors in judgment, remember that making a mistake marks you as a member of the larger family of humanity, because no one gets through life without some kind of miscalculation. When you choose self-acceptance as a way of life, you can have a more peaceful life.

Begin a period of quiet visualization with several cleansing breaths—inhale through the nose, exhale through the lips. Breathe in light, breathe out negativity and darkness. Call upon your Higher Self to step forward to answer a question. Pose the question: what wisdom, insight, or advice do you have for me today (or for this problem, or for the choice I must make)? When the answer comes, know it is because you are tapping into your own inner wellspring of wisdom.

Do a Daily Dive Into Peace

- Push away negativity.
- Draw in peace through aromatherapy and affirmations for inner peace.
- Plunge into a meditation of peaceful consciousness.

Claim Peace for Your Life

- Practice self-acceptance.
- Work with a soul symbol for peace.
- Use a meditation app for peace.

Open Yourself to the Endless Flow of Peace

- Release control and the need for perfection.
- Block peace-threatening energies from others.
- Take a negativity break.

Access Peace from Where You Are

- Find peace in art.
- Spend time in solitude and nature.
- Walk in the rain.

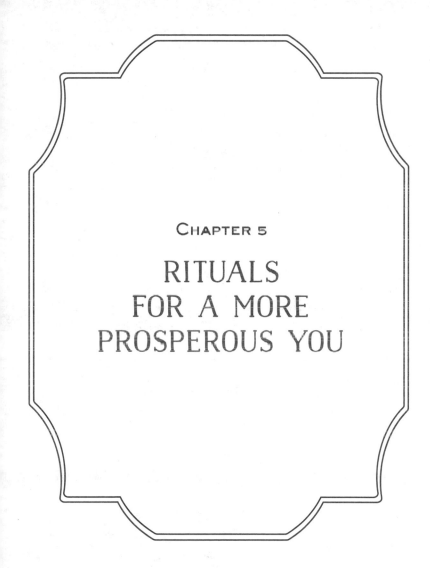

CHAPTER 5

RITUALS
FOR A MORE
PROSPEROUS YOU

You've probably heard friends lament that they wished they didn't have to work so hard for a paycheck that barely covers the bills. They do not realize that their prosperity (or lack of it) originates with their attitudes about money. Attracting prosperity involves shifting the paradigm of how you think, talk, and feel about money so it reflects positives, possibility, and abundance rather than focuses on negativity and lack.

According to the ancient universal law of attraction (or abundance), like attracts like, meaning that your thoughts are always attracting to you what you are thinking about most. If you're obsessing about the lack in your life and your struggles, you will attract more of that. Thinking about abundance, however, can draw more of it to you. Break down almost anything into its lowest form and you'll get energy and information. From a quantum physics perspective, your thought energy literally shifts particles of the Universe to create your physical life. When you realize that your mind isn't separate from the mind of the Universe and your body isn't separated from the body of the Universe—that all in the visible world is connected to the energy matrix of the invisible world, you begin to understand that your thoughts, words, and actions have powerful energy that can draw into your life what you want.

RITUAL 61.
ELIMINATE THOUGHTS OF LACK

Embrace Abundance

When you have an abundance of good health, you possess a positive attitude, mental acuity and alertness, physical well-being, and exuberant energy. An abundance of wealth suggests money is plentiful in your life—you don't fear losing it or having to struggle. Money is energy, and your thoughts are the magnet that draws money to you. When you understand this fundamental premise, you can release all thought of lack, struggle, worry, and fear. Instead, create a consciousness of abundance in all areas of life, including financial prosperity. Use the scent of herbs to remind you to return again and again to prosperity consciousness. Certain herbs associated with financial abundance include lavender, basil, mint, and cinnamon.

Mix together a pinch of dry basil, lavender, mint, and cinnamon in your wallet or a pouch in which you keep your paper money. Daily, open your wallet, move around the money, and let the scent remind you to repeat an affirmation such as, "I attract prosperity; my life is filled with abundance, and my needs are met." When you replace thoughts of lack with abundance and keep positive prosperity thoughts at the forefront of your mind, you set up an energy attraction for prosperity to flow to you.

RITUAL 62.
WRITE A BLESSINGS LIST

DISCOVER THE PROSPERITY THAT'S ALREADY YOURS

Laughter, love, health, friends, family, money, spiritual growth, and a loving and powerful support network represent a cornucopia of blessings that suggest a prosperous life. In fast-paced work environments that characterize the modern world, you might not realize how blessed you are. Almost every culture has rituals and symbols to draw abundance. An Eastern tradition is to hang in the northeast corner of a home or business a *yantra* (or mystical diagram) representing Lakshmi, goddess of wealth, or Shree Kubera, mentioned in the Vedas as the Ruler of Wealth and Riches. The northeast corner is also known as Eshaan corner, a highly energized space for worship.

Inside a red envelope, write a list of your blessings. Insert a dollar. Close the envelope and rub it between your palms to generate positive energy that will attract more of the same. Place the envelope in a northeast corner of your sacred space. Intensify the energy by placing a crystal on top of the envelope and cover both with a red cloth. Each week during the year, open the envelope, review, and add blessings to your list. Shake the dollar and the red cloth, and reassemble as before as you recite: "I attract an abundance of all good things that bless me and mine."

RITUAL 63.
SPRAY A SCENT OF SUCCESS

Draw Prosperity In

Success in large measure might better be referred to as affluence that comes from the Latin *affluere*, which means "to flow abundantly." If your vision of success is a virtual flood of riches, then head out to a candle store and pick up three cinnabar-scented candles, or make your own using wax, wick, and essential oil. While you are at it, purchase a little scented spray to freshen the stale money or wealth sector of your home. Don't know where the wealth sector is located? Find it on the ancient bagua map used in feng shui, the Chinese art of placement. Remove the clutter to create open space. This encourages the flow of money into your home. Add green color in the space to remind you of money. Move in a money plant, which might have an auspicious red string or ribbon tied around it.

Each day, check the health of your plant, tidy the room, light the candles, and spray a mist of cinnabar. Breathe in the scent of success and affirm: "Prosperity abundantly flows to me, blessing my life so through my affluence I may bless the lives of others."

RITUAL 64.
ATTRACT ABUNDANCE WITH CITRINE

PROSPER WITH THE
POWER OF YELLOW

As quartz goes, citrine (in hues of warm yellow to champagne, smoky shades, and deeper reddish tints) is a stone that is lovely to look at and also is believed to hold powerful energy. In crystal folklore traditions, citrine supports efforts of good health and sexuality. The quartz's sunny tint reportedly relieves depression symptoms, fosters a happy disposition, and helps assuage emotional swings. Citrine has been associated with the solar plexus chakra (Manipura). Because the stone reportedly governs success and prosperity and dissipates negative energies, it's been called the "merchant's stone" and the "money stone."

Citrine is a popular jewelry choice and you can find it made into earrings, rings, pendants, and pins. Before putting on your citrine jewelry—which, of course, you will wear to attract and magnify prosperity energy—cleanse the stone with soap and water, rinse, and thoroughly dry before wearing. After putting the gemstone jewelry on, say the following affirmation: "I love and accept myself as worthy to wear this powerful stone. I am drawing wealth to me." When you remove the stone, wrap it in fabric and store it in a box lined with fabric such as velvet.

RITUAL 65.
ACCESS THE WEALTH GODDESS

SUMMON THE POWER OF WEALTH SYMBOLS

If you were to imagine yourself as a wealth goddess, what would be your symbols? Call upon the power of wealth symbols to set up an energy attraction for the manifestation of financial prosperity. Choose from numerous diverse symbols of wealth found in many cultures throughout the world. Find bracelet charms of the symbols with which you most associate ideas of prosperity. Let them serve as visual stimuli to trigger thoughts of financial opportunities and prosperity showing up in your life. When you fashion and wear jewelry that incorporates charms symbolic of wealth, your thoughts better focus on attracting prosperity and creating more of it. Belief becomes reality.

Make a charm bracelet (or other piece of jewelry) with charms symbolizing wealth. For the bracelet, you'll need strong threading material, charms, and a simple clasp. Find these in the jewelry-making section of a craft store. Each day, slip the bracelet onto the wrist of your right hand. Place your left hand over the bracelet as you mentally recite an affirmation of gratitude and another for attracting wealth: "I am thankful for the wealth I already have. I place no limits of the quantity of money I am earning or the amounts I am attracting." Repeat this mantra throughout the day and also as you remove the bracelet at day's end.

RITUAL 66.
IMPRINT YOUR SUBCONSCIOUS

DISPLAY CURRENCY
AND COIN IMAGES

If you want more money, you have to impress upon your subconscious the idea of that money flowing toward you and ever circulating in your orbit. Trust that the bank of the Universe has plenty of money for your requests and know that the money coming to you doesn't mean someone else is not going to get theirs. That's not the way the ancient law of attraction works. Surround yourself with images of money to remind you to focus on abundance and the positive flow of energy that will attract prosperity.

Spend fifteen minutes each day with your eyes closed, your body relaxed, and your mind visualizing financial freedom. Imagine stacks of hundred-dollar bills banded in quantities of thousands of dollars. See these stacks covering the entire surface of the largest table in your house. Feel strong and positive emotion about claiming that money as you say the following: "I choose to bring into my life now [name an amount of dollars]." Say this affirmation thirty times each day for the next month or two. When opportunities begin to show up as indications that your subconscious is guiding you toward achieving your goal, give thanks and take advantage of those opportunities to create wealth.

RITUAL 67.
KEEP MONEY CIRCULATING IN YOUR ORBIT

Pay It Forward

When you want to achieve success in your business or other important areas of your life, it helps to cultivate a persistent desire and align your thoughts, emotions, and actions with that desire. A mind body spirit working together in harmony can achieve a quicker result than if you are in conflict. What you think about most is what you put the most effort toward achieving. Thoughts and actions are energy that set up positive, negative, or neutral reactions. Expressing gratitude for money in circulation smooths the way for more money to show up. An act of generosity further intensifies that likelihood.

Each morning as you prepare to pay for coffee in the drive-through, feel the plastic credit card or paper currency in your hand. Notice the sensation of weight and then weightlessness as you pay and weight again as the card or change comes back. Buy a cup of coffee for the guy driving the car behind yours. Let your emotion wrap around how good it feels to be able to bless a total stranger. Hold on to the feeling of gratitude and carry it into your day. Watch as money is showing up in your life as you begin to shift the status quo. During the day, whenever you hold a coin or currency in your hand, say, "I am a money magnet. Money flows easily to me from the Divine Source through the people, institutions, and organizations of the world."

RITUAL 68.
USE FENG SHUI

Shift Into Abundance Alignment

Feng shui ("fung shway," meaning "wind-water") is the ancient Chinese art of harmonious placement of objects in your home, office, or landscape to achieve optimal flow of qi (pronounced "chee," meaning "life-force energy"). Practitioners believe that you can create an energy attraction that brings prosperity, health, luck, and peace when you live according to the principles of feng shui that stress living life in balance with the earth. Find a printable bagua map on the Internet. Listed at the map's base are three areas: spiritual growth, career, and helpful people. Hold the map parallel with the floor and stand at your front door facing into your home and determine where the prosperity area of your home is relative to the bagua. Go to that area.

- Clear the clutter and clean the space.
- Move in a live plant (no spikey leaves, bonsai, or cactus) and a tabletop water fountain with three metal coins tied in red string or a frog with a coin in its mouth.
- Light and gently wave in all areas of the space a white sage smudge stick, reciting the following affirmation: "I sanctify this space with positive energy and feel grateful that now money easily flows in here and remains for the good of this household."

RITUAL 69.
GET OUT YOUR CHECKBOOK

WRITE A CHECK TO YOURSELF

Writing an abundance check to yourself might take only a minute or two of your time, but it could pay off substantially in a newfound prosperity. Consider how it's worked for others such as actor Jim Carrey who—as the story goes—wrote himself a check for $10 million that he carried around before he became a household name. Writing a sizable check taps into the law of attraction that postulates that all things you want or need are drawn to you from the Divine Source when your mental and emotional energies are aligned with appreciation and gratitude, love, generosity, and trust. Do the new moon check ritual once a month.

- On a blank check (a real one or one you create to look real), write today's date.
- Make it out to your full legal name.
- Leave blank the dollar amount box and line but on the signature line, write: *Law of Abundance*.
- Write in the memo sector: *Paid in full*.
- Take out the check at the beginning of each new moon and hold the paper in your palms while you visualize the dollar amount you desire to attract that month.
- Feel happiness when you are inspired with ideas for opportunities for making money as well as when money flows in; don't forget to express gratitude (write thank-you notes and tuck them into a box where you keep the check).

RITUAL 70.
PUT ON YOUR MILLIONAIRE'S MINDSET

PUT THOUGHT ATTRACTION TO WORK

Aim for thirty minutes each day to quiet your mind and to let go of limiting beliefs. Invite your Higher Self to inspire you with ideas on how to generate more revenue streams in your life. Gear up your "I am" statements to reflect abundance. For example, "I am abundantly blessed by the Universe [or the Divine, Source, or God]. I am a vessel eager to receive all good things. I am worthy." Paste up images or symbols that reflect your view of wealth. Zero in on a specific wealth intention such as a higher salary, increased amount for a contract, or an unexpected financial windfall. Believe that you are a magnet for abundance. Open an interest-earning savings account to receive money as it begins to arrive.

Three times each day hold a symbol of wealth (such as a silver dollar or gold coin) in your hands and gently rub your palms together while repeating the following affirmation three times: "Thanks to the Universe, I am manifesting boundless and limitless prosperity." To magnetize the affirmation, feel worthy and cultivate genuine joy and gratitude. Trust implicitly that your prosperity is on its way.

RITUAL 71.
NOTE THE VALUE IN YOUR LIFE

PUT VALUE ON THE
LIVES OF OTHERS

Noticing the ways your life imparts value to others and brings blessings upon you creates a spiritual lens for viewing prosperity. When you work energetically for abundance to clear away old mental tapes and emotional baggage, you make it possible for energy that's been impeded or stuck to shift. Positive thinking, energetic and enthusiastic action, and a sense of personal worth bring empowerment. When you want abundance, power, wealth, and recognition, the secret is to give first and then hold up your basket to the Universe to receive.

Purchase or make a receptacle such as a brass pot, a crystal bowl, a lovely basket, or a decorative box to hold treasures that show up in your life. Devise a ritual that magnetizes this container with abundance-attracting energy. For example, dip your finger into running water and run it around the rim or opening of your receptacle. Hold the bowl, basket, or box up and ask for blessings to surround, permeate, and fill the bowl for your highest good that you might use the gifts to bless others.

RITUAL 72.
CREATE A VISION BOARD

DEPICT THE ABUNDANCE YOU DESIRE

Your words, thoughts, emotions, and mental images—all have a potential to shift your life in a different direction. You might have heard of or even created a vision board to solidify ideas for a project or something you wanted to focus on with intensity. To create a whole new reality, create a vision board using the bagua sectors borrowed from feng shui. On a large piece of poster board draw three rows of three boxes each (nine equal boxes). Starting at the bottom, label the boxes left to right as knowledge, career, and helpful people. Next row up, starting on the left side, label the boxes: health, balance, and creativity. Label the final top row starting on the left: money, fame, and love. Cut and paste images that reflect for you abundance relative to each box. The idea is to create a vision for the life you want with a focus on what you can see, you can manifest. Put your vision board next to your desk.

Each morning or night (or both), hold the board and study the boxes, adding other images to them as you're inspired. Feel happy and excited and worthy. Trust that what you see you are going to get. Affirm: "I welcome abundance that flows easily to me for every sector of my life. May every living being and creature receive abundantly from the Universe."

RITUAL 73.
GATHER A CIRCLE OF FRIENDS AROUND YOU

FIND ABUNDANT FRIENDSHIPS

Friends influence your life in powerful ways, from helping you establish the direction you're headed to shaping your sense of self. With friends, you live longer, improve mental acuity, and expand your interests. Often, it is through friends that you find a mentor or meet a romantic partner. In friendship, you often align with others like you. However, you might benefit even more by choosing friends from diverse cultural and socioeconomic backgrounds because they expand your knowledge of the world. Think of your friends as your life's support network. Honor them with your loyalty, support, and compassion, but don't be afraid to weed out those demanding too much time and using your friendship only to vent stress. Celebrate and nurture the abundance available to you through friendship.

Once a month, gather with friends to eat and discuss a single deep question (philosophical, spiritual, or on a topic that forces everyone to delve into themselves for insights). Write your question on paper. Hold the paper in your hands. Read it to those gathered to start the discussion. Let food nourish your bodies, a ritual question nourish your minds, and the regular gathering strengthen the bonds of friendships.

RITUAL 74.
PURSUE INNER WEALTH

MAKE IT BENEFIT OTHERS

Imagine that within you is an infinite power that you can call on at any moment for what you need. Trusting in a higher power can confer what you need when you need it when you have let go of all ego-based fear, doubt, and skepticism. Your natural state is one of abundance, regardless of what circumstances you might currently find yourself in.

To shift your consciousness from stress, strife, and struggle, try some essential oil therapy. The greatest treasure you'll ever possess is knowledge of your true Self. When you access that knowledge, power and potent gifts are yours to use for good in the world.

- Light a candle to symbolize banishing of all darkness and negativity.
- Use four scented oils—sandalwood, myrrh, spikenard, and frankincense—and place two drops of each into a small dish and mix together.
- Saturate a cotton ball with the mixture and wave it beneath your nose.
- Call upon the Universe to guide you deeply inward as you gaze at the point between your eyebrows.
- Ask how you can use your abundant gifts of spirit and intuitive powers to help others.

RITUAL 75.
HANG A CHIME

Install a Dangling Wish-Fulfilling Jewel

In Asian spiritual texts, architecture, and culture, the wish-fulfilling jewel figures as a recurring theme of wealth and prosperity, appearing on roofs of temples, in spiritual iconography, and in garden ornamentation. The symbol is often created as either a dome-shaped object or a many-faceted gem. Bring this symbol into your home, office, or garden as part of a wind chime to invigorate wealth energy around you. You can integrate your jewel by tying or gluing it onto fishing line and attaching it to a chime hung near a window or a door. Imagine the breezes easily stirring its wish-fulfilling energy.

Hang the chime with your wish-fulfilling jewel in the wealth sector of your home or place of business. Upon arising and before your daily meditation, clasp your fingers around the wish-fulfilling jewel and take three deep breaths. Then sweep your fingers across the jewel and the chime's other hanging objects. Mentally recite: "As my intention moves the objects of this chime and stirs the jewel's wish-fulfilling energy, I am attracting wealth into my life."

RITUAL 76.
USE THE POWER OF IMAGINATION

REIMAGINE YOURSELF LIVING A PROSPEROUS LIFE

When you can clearly envision living your life in a new, more prosperous way, you start to believe it's possible. Help yourself buy into that belief by taking Selfies with the objects that represent abundance or prosperity to you. Perhaps they include expensive objects such as art, designer clothing, or an expensive car. Let these pictures help you clarify your personal image of an abundant lifestyle.

Set aside fifteen minutes each day to ritually daydream about yourself living your abundant life. In what way does that life look different from the life you already live? If it helps you to gain clarity for this daily ritual, take one afternoon each week to visit high-end stores where you take cell phone pictures of things you dream of owning. If you love clothing and desire to dress for the job you want (not the one you currently have), try on an expensive suit or dress that fits your newly imagined image of a wealthy you. Compile a photo montage in a journal or on a poster board. Use these images to clarify and magnify your daydreams. As your daydreams draw into focus what your abundant life looks like, set intentions, establish goals, become receptive to opportunities that show up, and take action. When your life is prosperous, use your ritual daydream minutes to see others prosper too.

RITUAL 77.
NURTURE OTHERS TOWARD THEIR GREATNESS

ACTIVATE INNER WEALTH

When you help others achieve their inner greatness, you are activating your own inner wealth, which affects wealth and abundance across all other spectrums of your life. Celebrating the wonderful attributes and inner power of others creates a mirror for viewing your inherent gifts. Certain attributes and skills such as attentiveness, problem-solving, and perspicacity can help achieve dreams and also foster inner resilience. Pointing out greatness in others, you lift yourself. Great doesn't mean flawless or perfect. It's a waste of time focusing on flaws—whether someone else's or your own. When you show such a generosity of spirit toward others, you increase your self-worth and confidence, which then magnetizes the energy of prosperity. You show your great wealth is in your heart, not your status or financial wealth (although a generous spirit attracts those too).

Light a prosperity candle (green-colored). Write down on paper what you desire and be specific. Fold the paper three times and place it a bag or keepsake box (colored purple for wealth, if possible). Scent a cotton ball with three drops of bergamot oil. Create an affirmation that focuses on your most successful attributes. For example: "I am smart, detail-oriented, capable, and worthy to receive _____ [insert your desire], which is on its way to me. I give thanks to the Universe."

RITUAL 78.
SHIFT YOUR MINDSET

LISTEN TO PROSPERITY TAPES

If you do a speed-walk around the park over your lunch hour, bike between buildings on your work's campus, or commute between cities to work, use the time to adjust your mindset about money. Listen to audiobooks by wealth and abundance experts via your earbuds and MP3 player or smartphone or insert a CD in the car player. As the conscious mind learns and begins to believe that "I deserve to prosper," the subconscious mind will echo the belief. Even the Buddha held that laypeople could live prosperous lives and become wealthy. He encouraged them to be successful. The revered sage, however, advocated that those acquiring wealth had an obligation to use their prosperity toward a wholesome purpose and gain that wealth in an honorable and ethical way, without deception or harm.

Make your smartphone and prosperity audiobooks integral to your early-morning run. As you warm up your muscles, recite the affirmation: "Money is my friend. Every day, in every way, money is flowing to me." Don your gloves against the early-morning chill and head out. Feeling the earth's support beneath your feet as you advance along your course, imagine how your "friend" money is always available to you.

RITUAL 79.
SHARE WEALTH POSSIBILITIES ON A DAILY BASIS

SHARING WHAT YOU KNOW CAN LEAD TO MORE OPPORTUNITIES FOR PROSPERITY

Whether or not you realize it, you begin to attract wealth possibilities from the moment you first put your mind to having more of what you want and less of what you don't want in life. Wealth possibilities emerge as the result of your intentions, new opportunities through associations with people you know, new contacts with inspiring new ideas, and many other ways. Prosperity can start showing up in synchronous events as a result of your resolve. Although your friends and business acquaintances may not know how to use rituals, affirmations, intentions, goal-setting, personal effort, and feelings of gratitude to attract wealth, they will likely support you in your endeavors. You, in turn, can share your knowledge about how the process can benefit them and at the same time reinforce your own efforts, thus bringing even more prosperity possibilities.

Begin a daily morning ritual by lighting a green candle (for wealth and illumination). Feel centered and grounded. Direct your thoughts inward and focus on a relative, friend, business associate, or someone else you'll meet today who could benefit from greater prosperity and be receptive to your ideas and efforts. Consider ways to open a conversation about attracting wealth. How will you offer to share knowledge and support him or her in the event that person chooses to embark on the path to prosperity with you? Think of ways you could support each other's efforts. Consider ways you could join forces to make money. Helping others helps you.

RITUAL 80.
SEEK SERVICE FIRST

YOUR ACT OF GIVING OPENS YOU TO RECEIVING

Wandering mendicant monks in India, Nepal, Thailand, Burma, and elsewhere have basically two possessions—a robe and an alms bowl. With great faith, they set off each day to share their faith and to receive what others are moved to give them. Rice and other foodstuffs, fruit, incense, or a flower might be dropped into the bowl. Neither the giver nor the receiver holds power over the other. It's a free exchange in which each benefits the other. One is served through the offering of a gift in a bowl; the other is served by receiving spiritual guidance and sustenance. In some instances, the transaction happens gracefully in silence. The giver knows the monk carries the bowl beneath his robe and is aware of meal times of the day. Nothing need be said. The act of giving opens the way for receiving. Consider what gifts might come into a bowl that you have designated as your spiritual alms bowl.

Think of your alms bowl as an abundance bowl. Place a few grains of rice and a flower in the bowl. Sprinkle it with a few drops of water and offer it to the Source. Throughout your day, let this bowl remind you of the generosity of the Universe and draw you into deeper service to others, thereby strengthening the inflow of abundance.

Abundant Attitude

- Embrace abundant thinking.
- Count your blessings.
- Surround yourself with the scents of success.

Prosperity Forces

- Work with powerful crystals such as citrine.
- Invoke the goddess of wealth.
- Imprint prosperity on your subconscious.

Abundance in Action

- Magnetize money through your good works.
- Align with abundance energy.
- Develop a millionaire mindset.

Align with the Law of Prosperity

- Install an abundance receptacle.
- Create an abundance vision board.
- Cultivate inner abundance.

Abundant Environment

- Hang a prosperity chime.
- Play prosperity tapes.
- Offer abundance possibilities to others.

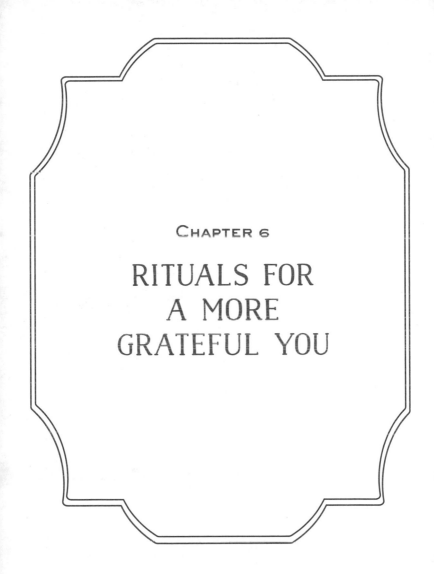

CHAPTER 6

RITUALS FOR
A MORE
GRATEFUL YOU

How often do you count your blessings and feel thankful for all the good you see in your life? If you didn't answer "often," you might want to incorporate the practice of being thankful into every day. Research shows that people who experience and express gratitude tend to feel more positive about life and often achieve levels of success that might elude less-grateful people. The reason has to do with how closely gratitude is linked to optimism and happiness.

People who mentally and emotionally experience gratitude are acutely aware of what's glorious about life and reap the benefits of holding and expressing an attitude of gratitude. Their appreciation of their triumphs and successes seemingly attracts opportunities for more in a self-perpetuating cycle. When their emotional muscle of gratitude is powerfully linked to optimism, individuals gain stronger immune systems, more connectedness to others, a greater sense of positivity, and a sunnier outlook on life. In general, feeling gratitude imparts a sense of well-being, fosters better sleep, and is linked to having better relationships. Like experiencing shared rituals, expressing feelings of gratitude generates in you a sense of belonging. And that, too, is something to be grateful for.

RITUAL 81.
BREATHE GRATITUDE

FEEL GRATEFUL FOR THE LUNGS
THAT SUPPORT YOUR LIFE

You breathe to calm yourself down, and you breathe into a deepening yoga stretch. You catch your breath after wrestling the groceries into the house or chasing your muddy-pawed dog. You might have wonderful lungs that easily take in oxygen and exhale carbon dioxide. But for people who suffer from asthma and other breathing problems, being able to breathe without effort is never taken for granted. Breath connects you to the sacredness of all life. How often do you stop and thank the Universe for being able to breathe in life-sustaining air? Before you begin your walk or run with Fido or head out to the market, take a few minutes to mindfully focus on your effortless and automatic breathing.

Observe the sensation of air moving through your nose on inhalation. Notice the soft, warm sensation of exhaled air as it crosses your lips after having left your lungs and moved up your trachea and into your oral cavity. Remain mindful for a moment of the physical sensation of breathing. With concentrated focus, do three cycles of deep breathing. Mentally say "Thank" on the inhalation and "You" on the exhalation that is twice as long as the inhaled breath. Feel your heart and mind filling with joy and gratitude.

RITUAL 82.
PAY HOMAGE TO YOUR HANDS

WHISPER GRATITUDE FOR ALL YOUR HANDS DO

Hands are amazing parts of your body, functioning almost continuously during your waking hours. Even so, you may take them for granted, overlooking how great their contribution is to your life or seeing them as ordinary when they are in truth extraordinary. You use your hands to show affection, love, and comfort to others, perform oblations, break bread with friends and family, and soothe away pain. Without your capable hands, how would you care for the rest of your body, button your clothes, drive or bike or sail, earn your living, hold a book, play a lively or beautiful piece of music, climb a mountain, pluck or plant a flower, shield your eyes as you gaze at a bird in flight, fold them in prayer, or cradle your head as you lean back to contemplate the kaleidoscope of stars strewn across a midnight sky?

Wash and dry your hands. Massage a cream into your hands as you affirm: "I am thankful for my strong, capable hands that reveal my talents and gifts to the world and also nurture my body and soul in myriad ways."

RITUAL 83.
KEEP A GRATITUDE JOURNAL

Focus on What's Flowing In

When you want to focus on the positives in your life, a gratitude journal can be a powerful tool. Scientific evidence supports the notion that people who are grateful tend to be happier than those who aren't. When you focus on happiness-boosting activities that include random acts of kindness you do for others, it enhances your levels of gratitude. Maintaining such a journal can lead to greater optimism as you count your blessings. Write in the journal at least once weekly. Write three things for which you feel grateful or bring you joy. Add other positive observations, record synchronous events, and jot down inspiring quotes or happiness goals. Create a title for that day's entries. Look up gratitude affirmations or inspiring quotes on your computer and print them for inclusion in your journal. As the weeks progress, you can look back over your entries and feel uplifted and fulfilled by all the goodness in your life.

Purchase or make a journal. Rub your palms together to create energy as you hold in your mind thoughts of thankfulness and appreciation for the wondrous world. Hold your palms facing down over the journal to impart the positive energy into the journal.

RITUAL 84.
SOW SEEDS OF GRATITUDE

REAP A HARVEST OF HAPPINESS

Make gratitude a guiding principle of your life. Start by practicing mindfulness in the present moment. Let your senses of sight, smell, hearing, taste, and touch and your intuition inform you of the great power and blessing inherent in a single moment. Absorbed, you let go of doing and come into being. Joy rises spontaneously in you but because you are so focused you might not realize how happy and satisfied you feel. Even more marvelous is that you lose your sense of individuality and worries fall away. To be able to practice mindfulness is itself a gift. This ancient practice can lead you to appreciate the interconnectedness of all life and a desire to acknowledge all the goodness that exists in every single moment. In turn, such feelings of gratitude for how you are blessed can trigger a desire to help others find happiness.

Use a small stone with the word *gratitude* printed on it as a touchstone to remind you to use positive language and say thank you often. Carry it in your pocket so that throughout the day whenever you touch it, you'll be reminded to sow seeds of gratitude.

RITUAL 85.
EXPRESS GRATITUDE AT HOME

SHOWER THOSE WHO LOVE YOU
WITH APPRECIATION

Don't miss the opportunity to express a thank-you to people you love and who love and support you—your family. If you feel appreciation when someone clears the dinner table, takes out the trash, or puts a load of towels in the washer—thereby easing your workload that might already demand you take a thousand steps a day—tell that person how much you are grateful for his or her efforts. When you assume that your gratitude is understood and no words are needed, you are robbing that person of a gift that could mean the world to him or her. Offer him a hug. Tell her with genuine sincerity how important she is in your life. Show love and appreciation at every opportunity; even when others aren't around, you can reinforce your attitude of gratitude.

Pluck a leaf of rose geranium and hold it beneath your nose. Breathe in the calm as you close your eyes and say a prayer thanking the Universe for those who love and support you and whom you cherish. Set off on a walk. Mentally call forth each person whom you love and tell them "Thank you for being in my life." Feel grateful that they are walking through the journey of life with you.

RITUAL 86.
SHOW GRATITUDE THROUGH AHIMSA

Practice Non-Harming

Ahimsa, many believe, is the foundation for the path of yoga. The word is derived from Sanskrit, meaning "not to harm." In India, the practice of non-harming or nonviolence is considered a cardinal virtue for Hindus, Buddhists, and Jains. The sacred text, the Chandogya Upanishad, dated from the eighth or seventh century B.C.E., lists ahimsa among the five essential virtues that also include truthfulness, sincerity, charity, and penance. In practice, ahimsa dictates that you view all living beings (humans, animals, and all life forms) as a reflection of the Divine. Speaking ill of another, criticizing, or engaging in dark thoughts about another only injures the self. Therefore, you must take care to do no harm to other creatures through your thoughts, words, or deeds.

Consider switching to a vegetarian, vegan, or raw food diets, but check with your physician first. Purchase an assortment of colored vegetables. Before you start prepping them, hold an assortment in your hands and give thanks for the abundant Universe that provides the means for not harming another creature's life to nourish your own.

RITUAL 87.
VISIT AN ASHRAM

SATURATE YOURSELF
IN BLISSFUL GRATITUDE

An ashram—or a place where spiritual pilgrims visit to feel uplifted—can inspire you to feel grateful for the magnificence of nature, the diversity of cultures, and forays into the inner sacred realms you explore through the ashram's guru's guidance. Ashrams possess highly vibrational energy that can dramatically increase your insight and awareness. Many ashrams are situated near bodies of water; others are located in mountains dotted with caves long loved by yogis who have appreciated such lofty places of solitude for doing *sadhana* (spiritual practices). As a guest of an ashram, you may be expected to do some selfless service such as mopping a floor or cleaning up after a meal is over—tasks that also offer an opportunity to earn good karma. If you are viewing a travel video or documentary about an ashram or holy site, make a note of the specific steps in the patterns of daily devotion and ways of giving back to kindle feelings of gratitude in you.

- Sit before your home altar.
- Light incense and a candle.
- Ring a bell to announce to the gods you are present and grateful.
- Enter the temple of your heart; plunge into a moment of feeling deep and honest gratitude for the exposure to spiritual truths and all the ways these come (whether through travel, videos, books, or personal contact).
- Offer a daily praising of the glorious gifts of the Universe, seen and unseen.
- Guide your consciousness deeply inward; enjoy the bliss.

RITUAL 88.
WRITE A LETTER

HAND-DELIVER IT

Expressing gratitude is a skill that can be developed and honed with habitual practice. When you want to share your feelings of appreciation to someone for something he or she has done for you, write that person a letter. Words are meaningful but words on a page are so much more lasting. The receiver can take the letter out again and again to read it and feel lifted by your heartfelt words. Maybe you're someone who just isn't comfortable gushing to others about how much you appreciate what they've done for you. When you take the time to sit down and write a letter, you can focus on language and tone and style for how you want to convey your gratitude.

Use the letter method to thank a friend for bringing you chicken soup when you were sick or for sharing bounty from her backyard or letting you use an empty shed on his property for storage. A handwritten letter is much more personal than a typewritten one for the purposes of offering a thank-you. Designate a special pen for these purposes.

- Set out paper and take your pen in hand.
- Close your eyes and breathe deeply for three cycles.
- Gather your thoughts around your friend's selfless act.
- Feel gratitude rising and write from that energy.

RITUAL 89.
SEE WITH NEW EYES

CREATE A NEW LENS FOR LOOKING AT THE OLD AND FAMILIAR

Kindle the wonder and awe of a child who is seeing something for the first time to inspire feelings of gratitude toward commonplace things in your world. Maybe you've never really noticed the massive old elm tree outside your office building whose canopy provides shade against the summer heat and drops its leaves in winter to let the sun heat the building's exterior and brighten the dark interiors. Or the way the snow glistens in moonlight. Or the orb-spinning spider's intricate web that had as its beginning a single thread. Perhaps you could look through the eyes of a child at the full moon rising, the drops of rain in a puddle, or the rainbow's appearance in the sky after the storm and let the wonder rise in you to fill your heart with gratitude.

Use a red ribbon to hang a crystal from an eastern-facing window where it can act as a prism for the sunlight. Give it a gentle spin to bring dancing rainbows into your room. When you are having a down moment, go to the crystal and be reminded of the rainbows in your life for which you are thankful.

RITUAL 90.
PRAY OFTEN

INTENSIFY YOUR GRATITUDE PRACTICE

Praying often may already be something you do in private or with others in a religious or spiritual community. Research suggests that frequent praying fosters higher levels of gratitude. If you don't already pray on a fixed schedule, consider beginning and ending your day with prayer. Pray over meals. Pray when you're running errands in the car. When you're traveling on the subway, bus, train, or taxi, mentally pray between stops. Your prayers can be simple statements of gratefulness, phrased spontaneously and freely. Prayers need not be eloquent or formal. You don't even have to close your eyes, although shutting out sensual distractions can help deepen your focus and your emotional connection to the Source of your being.

Prayer has no requirements beyond a humble heart and faith that the prayer is received. It takes only a moment to contact the Source of your being within and utter a declaration of appreciation and thanks. Since prayer may be done during any moment of your day, consider taking a tea break each afternoon. Light a sage smudge stick to cleanse and consecrate the space around you and then clasp your hands together in prayer and whisper: "I appreciate the awesome gift of life."

RITUAL 91.
ANALYZE INTENTIONS
BEHIND YOUR GIFT

INSIGHT INSPIRES GRATITUDE

When you are the recipient of a good turn by others, take time to think about what in their hearts led them to give you that gift. Think about the motivation of the gift-giver and the timing. You might come to the conclusion that the decision of the gift-giver wasn't entirely whimsical but perhaps purposeful. You were chosen to receive for a reason—he or she wanted to bring you happiness. Ask yourself if the person had to pay a cost to give you that gift.

For example, if your gift was a jar of jam from the first ripe batch of apricots on your neighbor's tree, think about how much time your neighbor spent gathering, washing, pitting, and peeling the cots, mixing the fruit with other ingredients, stirring the pot, filling and processing the jars. This likely will bring a sense of deep appreciation.

Pour yourself a cup of tea and put your feet up. Reflect on the person who has done you a good turn. Sip your tea and come up with several ways you could repay the kindness. Act on one of them.

RITUAL 92.
BE GRATEFUL FOR YOUR PETS

SHOWER THEM WITH LOVE

Consider yourself lucky if you have pets. Science shows owning a pet—such as a dog or cat—can improve your health by lowering stress and blood pressure. Dogs, especially, bring untold hours of goofy antics, sloppy kisses, playful shenanigans, and unconditional love. Cats are appreciated for their independence and tendency to snuggle up next to you for a nap, often lying in cute or contorted positions as they slumber oblivious to everything else going on in the household.

Dogs and cats might be the original social networking platform—they help you connect with other people like nothing else. Just petting them makes you feel grounded and anchored and less stressed. Your pet doesn't care that you had the worst day of your life at the office. He or she just wants to spend time with you. In turn, you can appreciate your pet for helping you live a longer, healthier life.

- Spend quality time with your pet each day, practicing mindfulness.
- Savor the sensations of your senses of sight, smell, touch, and sound.
- Watch your pet happily doing his thing, content to be with you in the here and now.
- Feel love and gratitude swell in your heart.
- Write about the mindful experiences of time spent with your pet.

RITUAL 93.
APPRECIATE YOUR
MATERIAL SUCCESS

COUNT YOURSELF FORTUNATE

Your material possessions hold meaning for you, some perhaps more than others. When you take stock of what you've earned or acquired, no doubt there are items you feel particularly blessed to own. There's nothing wrong with that. In fact, taking stock of personal possessions that you could never bear to part with can inspire renewed appreciation for how the items came into your possession and how happy—even secure—they make you feel.

You might have a treasured quilt that you pieced together with help from the arthritic hands of your grandmother before she passed away that now occupies a place on your bed and in your heart. Or your favorite piece might be a chocolate pot that you carried through Europe during your backpacking days. Or possibly your most cherished item is the *rudraksha mala* given to you by your teacher who said the Buddha wore the same type of beads. Having your items in a living space doesn't mean you always notice them with appreciation.

With an open heart, touch one item you love each day. Close your eyes and keep your fingers in contact with the item. If contact triggers a tender memory, be fully present with it. Affirm your gratitude for all you have.

RITUAL 94.
POST PICTURES ON SOCIAL MEDIA

Be a Beacon of Light

Social media keeps people connected as never before. It's how you can show your mom in the Midwest the photo of the scrumptious flourless torte you made using her recipe and for which you are grateful (since it always turns out perfect). When your best friend on the opposite coast wanted to see that new kitty you adopted from the local shelter, your pictures on social media brought an instant "like." And when an old friend from the past looked you up and made contact, it's because technology has made finding people easier than ever before. Social media is how you made six new friends in the last month. When you use social media, your world widens.

Since you are connected as never before, use the platform to express gratitude often. Having people comment on your posts can bring up positive feelings. In return, you can be an authentic beacon of bright light and positivity when commenting on other people's posts. Having fun with social media is a good thing when it makes you happy. But experts also warn that one of social media's downsides is a tendency toward passive consumption of other people's lives that can make you less happy with your own. So a great ritual might be to post something online every day of the year focusing on a blessing for that day for which you are grateful.

RITUAL 95.
PUT UP A BOUNTY
OF GRATITUDE JAR

FILL IT WITH NOTES OF THANKS

Jars are often filled with good things from a garden—succulent little jams in the smallest containers, relishes and tomato and pumpkin sauces in midsized jars, and juicy peaches and pears; not to mention green beans, corn, and all manner of squash picked at the peak of perfection—preserved in large ring-top canning jars. Dining on this bounty in the dead of winter kindles summer's warmth and memories that are sure to tug your heartstrings in appreciation. Put your trusty pen to paper and cultivate a bounty of gratitude.

Nail a particularly challenging yoga asana and feel over the moon about it? Write it down. When your significant other brings you chocolate and flowers just because, write about how happy he or she made you. After a period of meditation from which you emerge spiritually charged, note how blessed you feel. Write out your gratitude. All these notes get dropped into your garden jar of gratitude. Make your ritual into three parts: Pay attention to what shows up in your life. Notice how events, people, circumstances, and objects color your emotions, especially when something generates joy, peace, confidence, trust, and appreciation. Take time to write at length about these things through the lens of gratitude and then drop your notes into the jar.

RITUAL 96.
STRENGTHEN LOVE'S BONDS

Notice the Little Things

Studies show that romantic relationships are strengthened by gratitude. In a marriage, for example, when one spouse provides a thoughtful benefit for his or her mate, it creates a sense of gratitude and indebtedness in the receiver. The receiving spouse is reminded of the other's goodness, and this triggers happiness and other positive feelings. Thus, the bonds of the relationship are strengthened. Little thoughtful actions by both spouses increased relationship satisfaction, or gave what one study called a "booster shot" to romantic connectedness.

Every relationship has its ups and downs, but expressions of gratitude are a good predictor of upswings. In fact, it only takes the perception of caring behavior to get that booster shot. The gratitude one feels in a moment triggers a cascade of emotions. The positive effect of doing, saying, or noticing little things that benefit your romantic partner increases the happiness in your relationship and draws you even closer. You feel more deeply connected, loved, and valued. Make it your morning ritual to do a walking meditation or a sitting meditation with mindful breathing. Then when you are filled with peace and your heart is open, find one small thing that you admire about your partner and point it out with genuine appreciation.

RITUAL 97.
TAKE OUT THE OLD PHOTO ALBUMS

Bring On the Fond Memories

When you feel lonely or anxious or longing for something that you can't define, you might get out the old photo albums or boxes of pictures and start going through them. Soon you're back on a childhood camping trip with the family. Maybe you're visiting the missions in California for your middle school project, or getting help with your prom dress from your best friend before your date shows up. These feelings can give rise to gratitude as you realize that you've had family and friends who have loved you and maybe are still in your life and committed to your happiness. Researchers say that it's not uncommon for people to seek the positive emotional kick they get from a dose of nostalgia. It is a mood elevator. When you're feeling down, a little trip down memory lane can be a great compensating tool that you can use to come back into balance. Not only that, but it also energizes you and helps you feel connected.

Photos bridge the past with the present, reminding you of old friends and acquaintances whom you might have lost touch with. You might feel motivated to reach out and reconnect with them. As nostalgic feelings give rise to appreciation for the richness of your past, optimism for the present, and hope for the future, gratitude arises. Use such positive feelings as a departure point for journaling about all that comes up for you around your nostalgia.

RITUAL 98.
HANG A WHITEBOARD WITH PENS

WRITE ON IT DAILY

Make the expression of gratitude a family affair by hanging a whiteboard with different brightly colored marking pens in your home's common area where family members congregate. Make sure everyone knows where the board hangs and encourage them to take a moment each day to write on the board. Amid all the stress and negative news in the world, the board becomes a positive communication device, reflecting your deep heartfelt appreciation for the good that you see and experience.

Since all family members are able to read each other's comments about what or who has made them happy and why they are thankful, the whiteboard comments present departure points for further discussions about gratitude with your spouse, children, and even friends who happen to see the entries. Life is short, and children grow up all too soon. You might want to capture some of those entries in your cell phone picture gallery to remember them, since wiping the board erases them. Make the following your daily writing ritual.

- Take several cleansing breaths.
- Feel centered, grounded, and focused.
- Reflect on who or what is the reason you feel grateful and why.
- List three gratitude items on the board.

RITUAL 99.
GIVE BACK

Pay It Forward

Almost everyone knows what giving back means. When someone does something for you, you give back in kind. Pay it forward means that when someone does you a good deed, you do something good for someone else. These acts of generosity trigger plenty of positivity, inspiring feelings of happiness and gratitude. At a drive-through coffee facility, one person buys her morning coffee and spontaneously decides to pay for the coffee of the driver in the car behind her. That triggers surprise and gratitude in the second driver, who decides to pay for the third. And so on down the line of cars, the ripple effect begins as one driver after another is paying for a coffee order for perfect strangers.

When you start a ripple effect with some small gesture, you don't always get to see where your action might lead. But do it anyway. Make it your daily ritual of giving back or paying it forward: offer change to someone short on bus fare. Help someone get the parking space you're about to leave. Buy lunch for a homeless person. Record these actions and your emotions in your journal. Feel inspired to do more.

RITUAL 100.
TAKE A GRATITUDE RETREAT

Sneak Off Into Nature

It's good to periodically discharge all the energy you take on during the day, whether you're a stay-at-home mom single-handedly dealing with the demands of kids, pets, mountains of laundry, meals to be made, and rooms to clean, or a hardworking professional who loves her job but collects lots of unwanted negative energy from stressful interactions with others. Even if your daily work life is not stressful, sneaking away for a little respite in nature to recharge is a healthy choice to make. It helps bring you back to your center and rebalances your emotions.

In nature's healing presence, your whole mind-body being shifts. Restlessness gives way to the ancient rhythms of swaying trees, of time measured by the slow advance of the sun across the sky, of the quieting of the songbirds' chirping as evening approaches, and of a lowering of dusk's veil over the landscape. Feel gratitude for the filling and emptying of your lungs. Smell the fragrant wilderness—sunbaked earth, plant detritus, pine and juniper. Or if it's winter, listen to the crunch of snow underfoot and its soft plunking from tree limb to the ground. Breathe deeply in mindfulness. Reflect. Let gratitude fill your heart. Hold on to the moment.

SACRED LIFE

- Feel gratitude for spiritual knowledge.
- Sow seeds of thankfulness.
- Develop a new lens for seeing gratitude.

SATURATED IN GRATITUDE

- Feel gratitude for your lungs.
- Appreciate the work your hands do.
- Share your heart's love.

GRATITUDE IN PRACTICE

- Avoid harming in thought, word, or deed.
- Venture into a higher vibration of gratitude with an ashram visit.
- Intensify your gratitude through prayer.

SHINE THE LIGHT OF GRATITUDE ON THE WORLD

- Write a personal note of thanks and appreciation.
- Shine the light of gratitude on social media.
- Encourage family-sharing of gratitude.

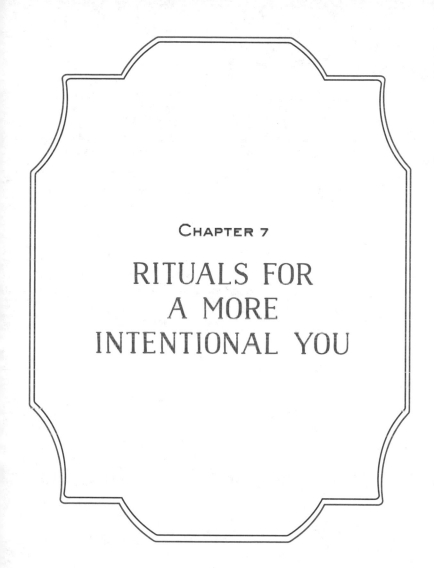

CHAPTER 7

RITUALS FOR
A MORE
INTENTIONAL YOU

Intention is a decision you make in the present that manifests in the future. It is more than a hope or a wish—neither of those are strong enough from an energy standpoint to manifest anything. Intention is a determination that you *will* accomplish a goal or *will* attract a person, circumstance, or thing that you desire. Forget the past; you can't change it. Embrace your present and consider what kind of future you want. Visualize yourself in your future life. Where you are, what you are doing, and how you are living and feeling? What's around you? Who's with you? Are you married or single? Working at what? Enjoying what type of hobbies? What's the most important thing about this future? Focus on forming a clear intention before you ask the Universe to manifest it. Once you have a goal or intention, you can begin to put together certain steps to claim your vision. All your effort—creative visualization, summoning powerful emotion, taking action, thinking and talking about your dream, and doing affirmations—combine to bring it to fruition. Too often, people don't see an instant result and give up. Don't shortchange yourself by doing that. If you truly want a successful result, be persistent.

RITUAL 101.
LEARN TO BE PRECISE

SAY WHAT YOU WANT
BUT WITH CLARITY

When someone asks you what you're going to do with your life, how would you reply? A lot of people move through their lives like automatons, acted upon by external circumstances and complaining about unexpected change and missing opportunities. Few of us live in isolation. Most people are surrounded by a lot of other folks—family, friends, coworkers, bosses, and others. These people all exert an influence on you. They're moving in a certain direction. Living an intentional life means you choose to stay in step with them or become intentional and move in an entirely different direction.

Let's say you don't like working in the public sector and instead want to devote your life to eco work that benefits the planet. Your dream meets with resistance from all but your closest friend, who supports your following your heart. What others say should matter less than what you desire. And what you desire, you can set for the intention of having. Set a time each day for renewing your intention. Breathe in. Breathe out. Say "Om." Make a specific declaration that uses clear language. For example, "I intend to live and work in a Midwestern eco-village where everything is shared and the village is organized around ecology and sustainability."

RITUAL 102.
SEIZE OPPORTUNITY
WHEN IT SHOWS UP

DISPLAY REMINDERS OF YOUR
INTENTION TO TRAVEL

You've always wanted to go to Peru, see the Andes, the Amazon rainforest, and Machu Picchu. Peruvian landscapes, colonial cathedrals, and ethnic works of art dot your walls. You can't explain the attraction since you don't know any Peruvians, nor have you had any other exposure to the country. Yet, when someone asks you where you'd most like to go on vacation that country pops right up on your lips. Write out your intention in a clear statement of purpose and then you are ready to break your purpose into smaller, incremental goals. Write those down and a reward for reaching each one. Follow this plan with the following affirmation: "I intend to visit Machu Picchu in May next year during the full moon cycle." Stay focused. Do not doubt and you'll get there, because every intention must be answered.

Here's a twice-daily ritual to strengthen your specific intention (in case it isn't going to Machu Picchu). Light a joss stick (of dried perfume paste) or incense to sanctify the space.

- Sit in your favorite meditation asana with eyes closed and declare your specific intention.
- Feel worthy. Trust that you've been heard.
- Visualize your desire manifesting and feel the emotional high.
- Seize opportunity when it comes; give thanks.

RITUAL 103.
BE YOUR OWN HERO

Do for Self What You Always Do for Others

You give generously of yourself and in myriad ways. You don't feel smug about it, you just do what you think ought to be done to help out—at school, work, church, and the various organizations you belong to as well as those in which your children are involved. You'd never fail your children or your spouse. So how about making some superhero commitments to yourself? The truth is that the person who can lead you to your best life probably doesn't wear a cape or a mask. Who is in charge of all you do, your actions, thoughts, emotions, deeds, and the direction you go in every day? Of course, it's you.

If you've been so busy with life's ups and downs that you can't remember the last time you took time just for yourself, it's long overdue. Create space in your life for you. Light a scented kitchen candle. Put on soft music. Make a cup of your favorite brew. Put your feet up. Wrap yourself in a soft shawl if you feel cool. Enjoy your beverage as you brainstorm many new ways you can carve out time to nourish your body-mind-spirit.

RITUAL 104.
FIND TRUE LOVE

MAKE YOUR LIST OF
WHAT YOU WANT

There's perhaps no greater longing than to find your soul mate, some-one who satisfies in you that sense that you are home in the spirit of his or her being. If you've tried to find that special someone and have given up, take heart. Maybe you're not asking the Universe in the right way. Actually, a useful analogy might be placing an order for boba at a bubble tea bar. You wouldn't tell the server to just give you whatever he or she feels like. You'd be specific: Japanese infused green tea with honeydew tapioca pearls with honey and served hot.

Giving the Universe an order for a soul mate means you have to be precise. What traits and qualities must your candidate have? What physical attributes? What personality type? Must he love children? Pets? What about fiscal responsibility? How important is emotional maturity? Make your list specific. If you are really ready, here's what you do. Take some cleansing breaths. Declare your intention with specificity. Make an affirmation: "I am ready to welcome my soul mate into my life." Visualize your soul mate showing up. Feel the jubilation. Clear a space in your life, and live as though your manifested desire is a fait accompli. Thank the Universe often and with sincerity.

RITUAL 105.
CREATE A NEW LIFE

VISUALS HELP YOU GET THE INTENTION RIGHT

If your life isn't working for you, change it up and make it visual. You don't have to feel trapped and stuck any longer. Begin work right now. Create a vision board for your dream life. Tape pictures of how you wish you were living instead of how you are presently getting through your days. Get your dreams up there on the board along with job types or a new career. If there's a radical move such as living abroad, put the new country on your board too. Add quotes, power words, and spiritual symbols. Seek new meaning for your life, as meaning gives you a direction, a focus, and a purpose. Call on the Universe to help you bring about a positive change.

Clear the clutter (physical and mental). Release regret, guilt, and attachment to elements of your old life. Make space for new energy as structures break down in your old life to create a fresh paradigm. Set your intention in writing so that you are laser-specific in what you want before you declare it aloud. Make strong and decisive affirmations that you repeat often throughout the day: "I am happy to be on purpose with my life. I deserve all the good that is coming."

RITUAL 106.
INTENTION FOR DEALING WITH PAIN

USE A BUDDHIST APPROACH

Pain, especially when it is chronic, can claim all the joy from your life as you suffer and seek relief from myriad sources. Chronic physical pain can take an emotional toll resulting in higher stress levels, a sense of hopelessness, and increased isolation. The Buddhist approach to pain is one of gentleness and kindheartedness. You practice loving-kindness toward yourself and determine to move toward the pain rather than trying to stuff, circumvent, repress, or suppress it. Use mindfulness to embrace pain's energy. Notice sensations within the pain. Do they arise and then recede?

Notice how the pain isn't one big solid block but lots of different sensations rising and falling. Also find a spot on your body that has no pain such as your big toe or heel that tells you that not all of you is in pain—just an area where sensations are splitting. The revered Vietnamese Buddhist monk and peace activist Thich Nhat Hanh says to let pain come in and care for it like a mother caring for her infant. Ring a small bell to remind yourself to stop, grow still, and feel intensely alive as you put your mind on the breath. Form an intention: "I will care for the sensations of pain with the energy of mindfulness." Do this ritual daily.

RITUAL 107.
CULTIVATE PERFECT HEALTH

Tap Aventurine

For many years now, science has embraced the idea of a mind-body integrated approach to health. Whereas Ayurveda has always used this approach, Western medicine has lagged. We learned years ago that the human body is a field that contains information, intelligence, and energy. In fact, the human body has 50 trillion cells that amazingly do the work of keeping us healthy. For healing to begin when a health issue arises, your mind needs only to put its energy on the affected area of the body.

Aventurine, a lovely green stone, can be a touchstone for your daily ritual for good health. Begin your practice of stillness by observing your breath for a few minutes. Touch the aventurine to your heart and tap it. Affirm: "I am mindful of my heart health." Touch the stone to your forehead. Tap and affirm, "I am mindful of my emotional health." Run the stone in a large circle in front of your body three times as though you are creating a web of healthy, healing energy. Set the stone aside and make an intention declaration: "I intend to do all I can every day in every way to stay healthy, happy, and fit."

RITUAL 108.
FIND YOUR DREAM JOB

CHOOSE A SYMBOLIC OBJECT TO REPRESENT YOUR DESIRE

There's nothing worse than having to play mind games to get up and go to work each day at a job you hate. If you find yourself in that situation, don't waste a minute more living your life in that mode. You could stay in that line of work, but it's pretty much a guarantee of early burnout and health issues to follow. If you don't know what line of work you'd be good at, consider types of activities that make you happy when you're doing them. Don't be timid. Go for what speaks to your passion.

Formulate a clear intention of the kind of job you want to manifest. Find some tangible object such as a car key if you want to design cars or work at an auto dealership, an egg cup if you want to be a farmer and raise chickens, or a packaged toothbrush if you want to work in a dentist's office. If you have loftier intentions, that's terrific. Just find an object that represents your dream job. Morning, noon, and night, hold that object in your hand and recite your intention. Feel it, believe it, visualize it, affirm it, and give thanks for it until the job shows up.

RITUAL 109.
SET AN INTENTION FOR YOUR YOGA PRACTICE

ADD SOMETHING EXTRA

Many yoga teachers ask their students to set an intention at the beginning of class. The intention becomes something a little extra for the student to work on that day. You can use the same principle for your private yoga practice. Dedicate your private exercise period to a quality such as strength of mind-body-spirit and push yourself to master some pose you haven't yet. Maybe it's the Wheel Pose (Urdhva Dhanurasana) or the Crane Pose (Bakasana). Yoga poses are all about strengthening and opening and healing what comes up. When you feel weak and vulnerable in one area of your life, it can affect other areas. Setting intention can help you focus so that you can work on strengthening your weakest area. It prepares you to take yoga from your mat into places of your life where you might have felt too vulnerable to go.

Mix two drops each of neroli, bergamot, and rose oil and vaporize it to eliminate negative energy from your space. Chant "Om" three times. Practice several cycles of mindful breathing. Make the prayer mudra at your heart with palms together. Declare your intention. For example: "I am a channel for strength and power and creativity."

RITUAL 110.
DECLARE INTENTION
TO BE A BETTER PARENT

GET HAPPY

Perhaps you grew up in a loving home with two parents who had exceptional parenting skills. Maybe they rarely if ever raised their voices or lost their tempers, and never became the anger they were trying to express. If that's the parenting lens created for you to gaze through, you can feel grateful that your parents truly blessed you. You've got a great example to emulate. Others have had vastly different upbringings. Regardless of how your parents raised you, you will face your own challenges with your children. Parenting classes can help. Raising children is not easy. Old wounds in your childhood can come up as your own child acts out. How you handle your emotions will dictate how you teach your children to handle theirs.

Drink a glass of clean, fresh water. Take a deep breath. Make a mental vow to be the best parent you are capable of being—that's the first step. Declare the following intention: "I am becoming an inspired and happy parent." Notice how your vibe seems lighter. Feel grateful for this. It means you will soon be drawing closer to your goal and the energy of the Universe will be a wind in your sail to help you.

RITUAL 111.
GREET YOUR GUEST AS GOD

KNOW ALL THINGS ARE POSSIBLE

In India, there is a tradition that when a stranger comes calling, you assume that guest quite possibly could be God and so you offer him or her the richest tasting tea (meaning it will have more milk than usual) and sweets. You invite your guest in and make him or her comfortable. This is a lovely tradition that brings the stranger into belonging with those in the home.

When you have been calling forth an intention for more help and a caring person shows up, you have to wonder whether the presence of this person is a gift of the Universe or a fluke. If your intention is still valid (you haven't given up on it), then your desire for help just might have arrived. Check back in with your intention. If your intention has been too fuzzy, it needs a little sprucing up with laser sharpness. Your ritual will be to reaffirm that all things in the Universe are possible, and then in the morning face the mirror and declare your refined, precise intention. If the caring and helpful person (formerly the stranger) is genuine, express gratitude to the Universe for answering your intention.

RITUAL 112.
WORK WITH DIET

Use Intention, Attention, and Information

Set an intention to lose, gain, or hold your weight and get healthier. Intention won't work if your subconscious doesn't believe your conscious thoughts. Affirm that you want to make lasting, unwavering dietary modifications to be healthy. With your attention focused on the dietary changes you need to make, choose one bad food practice to change until your choice becomes a habit. Don't try to change everything at once; it sets you up for failure. Keeping a journal will enable you to recognize triggers for unhealthy eating habits. You'll want to self-monitor for these triggers. Don't keep foods in the pantry, fridge, or cupboard that will tempt you back into old patterns. Write out several affirmations and repeat them often.

Another helpful technique is to view foods through a lens of healthy versus unhealthy. Remember that you want to make dietary changes to be healthy. Discover information about why certain foods are healthy and others aren't. Feel happy when you make good food choices. Know that by the choices you are making, your body is changing from the inside out. With knife and cutting board at hand, recite your intention before meal preparation: "I am making wise food choices to keep me fit for life."

RITUAL 113.
INTENTION FOR MORE WILLPOWER

ALIGN WITH THE DIVINE

You start out projects with the best of intentions of following through but sometimes it just takes more force of will than you have to see the endeavor to its end. In architecture, there's a stage at which something is presented to show what the end product will look like, but it isn't the end product. It's a small display model. When you are satisfied with presenting an incomplete or unfinished project instead of the final version, it may be because you already got the payoff—the compliments—so you don't feel motivated to go any further. This is unfortunate. Life isn't about presenting but starting and finishing. Follow-through takes willpower.

With a strong will, you can overcome any adversity. You can stand steady in the face of disease, life's challenges, and even misfortune. You can become highly creative and innovative. Success in any arena can be yours. To develop a dynamo will, strengthen it through the power of intention. Each morning, stand before the mirror. Rub your palms together until they are warm with energy. Place your palm over your heart and reaffirm your intention to have a stronger willpower than the day before: "Today, I am yoking my will to the infinite will of the Universe."

RITUAL 114.
GETTING ALONG BETTER WITH OTHERS

Work Your Smiles and Insights

A disarming smile is a good place to start when dealing with a difficult person. If there's someone in your workplace who doesn't have a good word for anyone and seems to enjoy baiting you, a smile might help turn things around. Keep a small bottle of lavender oil in your desk. When someone says something that is hurtful or thoughtless that you don't like, take a whiff. Your brain can't process anger and calm (two different emotions) at the same time, so the lavender can ease anxiety and soothe your nerves. It's also beneficial for cognitive function, as it increases mental activity.

Remove yourself from a situation where you feel yourself growing tense and perhaps confrontational. Studying people for insights helps you understand them better. Find out their interests and talk about those. Avoid engaging people who have a false sense of superiority. They might actually suffer from an inferiority complex. Dab lavender oil on your wrists and rub them together. Form the prayer mudra. Breathe deeply several times to calm and center yourself. Make an intention: "I get along with others by aligning myself with the infinite power of love."

RITUAL 115.
CONTROL YOUR EMOTIONS

ALIGN WITH A HIGHER POWER

Emotional swings are a part of life. There are the highs when you feel so full of joy that your heart can hardly cope with the emotion. But a bad situation can trigger a swing in the other direction. Despair can drop you to your knees and pain can block the light of hope, peace, love, and optimism. Psychologists explain emotional response as an appropriate or inappropriate reaction to an event. If you desire to create an intention to live more in control of your emotions, start by understanding what circumstances or people trigger your unwanted feelings. Plan ahead for dealing with a situation or meeting that could send your feelings spiraling off into anger or worry.

Try shifting your attention away from anger agitators to an activity that you can focus on instead. Change your thinking about the situation as well. Psychologists call this technique cognitive reappraisal, and simply explained, it means you reassess the way the situation is making you feel. Carry blue lace agate as a touchstone for harmony in your pocket. At home, light blue candles and place the stone nearby to diffuse discord and restore calm. When you need reassurance, hold the stone and make the following intention: "I align my heart with the infinite power to guide my emotions, intellect, and wisdom."

RITUAL 116.
CREATE BETTER KARMA

GIVE THE GIFT OF SELF

You might not be able to create a better world for all of us, but you can create a better world for some. In the process, you'll be generating some good karma. If you love children, do some volunteer work that benefits them. If you're a supercreative type, think about teaching art or theater to children at your local community center or through a park and recreation program. Or consider being a foster parent. Join a Big Sisters or Big Brothers organization and mentor someone.

Making a commitment to others to do something for their benefit allows you to be more intentional in the kind of karma you are creating. Your goodness won't go unnoticed. Others may be inspired by your example and follow suit. Many spiritual traditions teach that it's better to give than receive and that the purpose of life is to do service for others. When you give freely of yourself and make others happy, your own happiness will expand exponentially. You'll create some good karma. Your cup of joy will overflow. Begin and end your day with the following declaration of intention: "I intend to share my life with others, using my divine gifts for their highest good as well as mine."

RITUAL 117.
WORK FOR GLOBAL CHANGE

BE A LIGHT BEARER

You want live a more intentional life and make a positive difference in the world. Be guided by the power that comes from listening to your inner voice of reason and guidance. Spent time in meditation, seek soul guidance, and then use your power on the path you choose. Maybe your work will be volunteering on a Mercy Ship that brings healing and hope to the world's forgotten poor. Perhaps you'd like to work to end childhood hunger through an organization such as Feed the Children. Or maybe your heart's aspirations align with the emergency food and healthcare needed by the world's children in crisis and their mothers in developing countries.

Do a pranayama known as alternate nostril breathing (*Nadi Shodhana*) to calm the mind and balance the energies in your body. Sit in a cross-legged pose. Place your right thumb against your right nostril. Inhale through the left nostril. Close the left with your ring finger and release the right. Breathe out through the right. Close. Use thumb to close the right nostril. Breathe out through the left. This completes one round. Do two rounds. Meditate on being a light bearer on the planet. Make your intention declaration.

RITUAL 118.
BRING LIGHT TO YOUR ENTREPRENEURIAL DESIRE

Light an Intention Candle

Is this the year you'll launch your new creative venture? Take that master-level class to teach gardening, yoga, art, Ayurvedic massage, or cooking? Or maybe you've been thinking about forming a women's collective to produce fine handmade monogrammed linens. Whatever your dream is for your enterprise, don't hold back. Grab life with both fists and make that dream a reality. Use the power of intention to call to the Universe that you are ready to manifest that venture. Give yourself permission. Write that business plan. Find funding. Surround yourself with a can-do team. Brainstorm every aspect and possible scenario right down to the smallest detail before launching.

Purchase an intention candle to shine light upon a coveted projected or personal endeavor. A green candle symbolizes abundance and success whereas a yellow candle signifies the process of launching a plan. A red candle symbolizes courage and relationships, so important when you are launching a new venture. Choose your candle color. Sit before the candle to ground your energies. Write out your intention and place it under the candle. Light the candle and declare your intention. Say a prayer of thanks.

RITUAL 119.
BE A FORCE FOR GOOD
IN YOUR COMMUNITY

ASK A FRIEND ALONG

You see your community television channel advertising for volunteers to serve on one board or another. You've thought about it, but haven't taken any action. And yet, you like the idea of doing good things for your community. Maybe what's holding you back are the unknowns in the equation. You don't know how much time might be required. You don't know the others who might be serving, what the process is, or what else is involved. If there's a nagging little voice inside of you prompting you to call the number on the screen or visit city hall, why not encourage a friend to join you to go and find out.

Consider your excursion an excuse for lunch and a fact-finding mission. Public service isn't for everyone, but if it calls you don't hold back. Scent the space around you with rosemary to energize your mind and sharpen mental acuity. Gather a notebook, a pen, and perhaps a recording device along with your smartphone for notes, pictures, and video. Make your intention known to the Universe: "I offer my talents and skills to my community for my highest good and that of my fellow citizens."

RITUAL 120.
CLAIM YOUR DIVINITY

You Are a Child of the Divine

No one imprisons you in your life. Its smallness or expansiveness is truly all your doing. As easily as you wall yourself in from the wider world, you can throw open the gates, expand the frame that holds your image in this world, and embrace the infinite you in all its splendor and magnificence. What will it take for you to embrace and claim your divinity? You are a child of the Divine. Perhaps the truth is too awesome to wrap your mind around. You feel you can only handle that knowledge in small increments of time—a fleeting moment here; a longer one there. But through deep and mindful breathing, in meditation you can open your heart and mind to the truth—that you are that "I Am."

Light a candle. Sit in the lotus or half lotus. Deep breathe through several cycles. Make your intention: "I am a drop of water on the Ocean of Spirit." Listen to Deva Premal, a musician who perhaps is best known for her Buddhist and Sanskrit mantras, sing the Moola Mantra. Let the lovely music and word vibrations transport you to the exalted state of infinite love and unbounded joy.

SEQUENCES

HEALTHY INTENTIONS

- Speak your desire with precise language and with feeling.
- Act on opportunity when it shows up.
- Create space in your life just for you.

INTENTIONS TO MANIFEST YOUR DESIRES

- Find true love.
- Deal with pain.
- Get healthy.
- Find your dream job.

INTENTIONS TO WORK THROUGH DIFFICULTIES

- Strengthen your weakest areas.
- Be a better parent.
- Tackle your diet.

INTENTIONS FOR STRENGTH AND RESILIENCY

- Develop more willpower.
- Deal better with difficult people.
- Get a handle on emotional triggers.

INTENTIONS WITH FAR-REACHING POSSIBILITIES

- Create good karma and a life of sharing with others.
- Become a force for global change.
- Promote the greater good in your community.

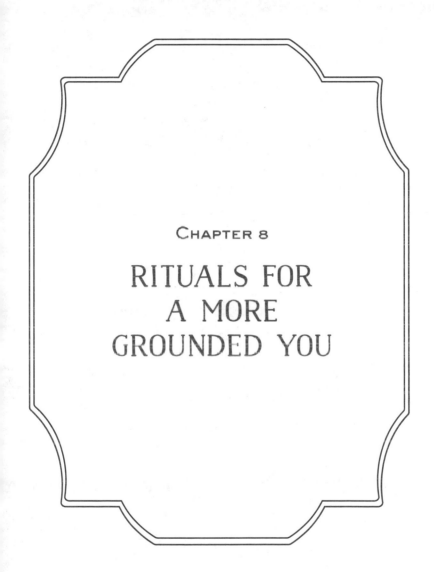

CHAPTER 8

RITUALS FOR A MORE GROUNDED YOU

Grounding means finding your center when any kind of emotional upheaval claims your sense of strength, steadiness, and balance. When you are in emotional conflict, it can feel as if you are losing your sanity. You might be remembering a troubling situation that occurred in the past. On the other hand, you could be sitting on a park bench perfectly immersed in peace when someone walks by and utters a thoughtless remark that triggers emotional reactions in those within earshot. Suddenly chaos ensues with a vengeance, and you find yourself reacting with feelings of agitation, panic, confusion, and chaos. Although it takes a little time for the "fight or flight" chemicals that have flooded your brain to diminish and a calm centeredness to return, there are things you can do to bring back equilibrium.

From stepping away from a challenging situation to facing unresolved inner conflicts in silent contemplation, there are many things you can do to become emotionally strong, steady, and balanced again. Whether you practice deep breathing, creative visualization, or yoga asanas to draw up the earth's energies, there are a variety of grounding rituals you can do to reestablish your emotional steadiness and balance.

RITUAL 121.
BECOME THE TREE ROOT

Build Balance Skills with Tree Pose

Balance, coordination, focus, and concentration are important attributes to acquire and hold on to as you age. All four are fostered in the beginning yoga pose known as the Tree Pose (Vriksasana). Keep your eyes open to help with maintaining balance. Practice this pose near the kitchen counter in case you need to reach for support. As you improve, do this pose outside near other trees. Use your imagination to feel as though you've become a tree, deep roots into the earth, head and hands stretching into the heavens.

1. Stand with feet flat and parallel, big toes pointing forward, sides touching.
2. Shift your weight onto the left foot.
3. Bend your right knee. Clasp your right leg at the knee or ankle with your right hand and lift and press the sole of your foot against your left calf. With practice, you'll aim for higher position on the left inner thigh near the pelvis. Keep your bent knee pointing right, not forward.
4. Breathe and find your balance.
5. Inhale and slowly bring your palms and fingers touching together at your heart center or over your head in the prayer mudra.
6. Repeat the process for the other leg.

RITUAL 122.
TOUCH YOUR TAPROOT

Focus Your Awareness There

Sometimes when you feel a little spacey and off center, the cause can be internal, such as hormone levels or medication. But you can also feel spacey in an unfamiliar environment where the energies are not in synch with your own. If you are empathic, other people's energies can feel unfamiliar and unbalanced. If you are in a situation where you are out of your element or feeling way out of your comfort zone, you can sense that you need to do something to ground yourself. Listen to your inner guidance for what is required. Drink a glass of fresh, clean water. Sit and be mindful of the imbalance and the energies you feel. Consider whether they are yours or someone else's.

Visualization can work wonders when you can't shake off the imbalances you feel. Find a place to sit where you can close your eyes and be safe. Put on a piece of smoky quartz jewelry or hold the stone in your hand. Visualize a root growing from your spine to extend deep into Mother Earth and through which you can draw grounding energies. Let these restore your peace and calm your thoughts if they are agitated or when you feel anger, hurt, self-doubt, or other negative emotional energy.

RITUAL 123.
RETREAT INTO THE PRACTICE OF MOUNA

LET THE YOGA OF SILENCE FILL YOU

Mouna is silence. When you stop speaking to observe silence, the energy of your vocalizations must find other expressions. You can use this energy to accomplish deeper spiritual work. In meditation, silence fills you. Many people can hear more intensely the *Omkara*, the primordial sound of the Universe vibrating as Om. If you haven't been able to hear it, try plugging your ears with your fingers. Close your eyes. Listen intently and deeply. Let the silence fill you. Lose yourself in the inner sound.

In India there is a kind of yoga known as shabd yoga or "the yoga of sacred song or sound." It emphasizes listening to the inner sound as if it is a river. The flow is quiet at first. The longer you listen, the stronger it becomes. That river can carry your consciousness to ever-higher levels until you drown in the bliss of that sound. Combine the sound with the inner light and you get surat shabd yoga (light sound yoga), a Sikh tradition. For a single day, practice the yoga of silence. Spend the day without intoning a single sound. Listen to the sounds of the inner world. Use a small handheld board if you are compelled to write messages without speaking. Feel how grounded and centered you become.

RITUAL 124.
ANCHOR YOURSELF

Feel Anchored Within

Sometimes it feels as if you can't catch a break. You fall behind on a project. Then your husband brings home the flu. You get it and develop severe bronchitis. If you thought you were going to get that project back on track, think again. You must pack your child's things for a school field trip tomorrow but first the laundry must be done. And suddenly because of the storm outside, the power goes out. Using the washer and dryer are out of the question. How do you recover from a nonstop assault on your peace and well-being? You find a way to ground and center yourself. You begin working from the inside out.

Take off your shoes and sit in a place where you can draw the earth's energies through your bare feet as they touch the grassy ground. Or curl up in front of the hearth and let the firelight dance on your face as you chant "Om."

- Light a ceremonial candle.
- Burn incense.
- Sit in a comfortable position and pay attention to your deep breathing cycles.
- Close your eyes and lift your inner gaze to the point between the eyebrows.
- Mentally chant "Om" on the breath in; a numerical count on the exhaled breath.
- Feel your sitting bones settle. Dive deeply inward into grounding and peace.

RITUAL 125.
TUNE UP YOUR
MULADHARA CHAKRA

BRING BALANCE AND
HARMONY BACK

The Muladhara chakra is also known as the root. It is located at the base of the spine. It can be blocked by unresolved low self-esteem and chronic tension. When you feel out of balance and need grounding, restore the balance of this center of energy. It helps you feel grounded with the earth as well as safe and secure and still. You will want to open and stretch your feet and leg muscles. Then move into Standing Forward Bend (Uttanasana). After that, move into the Head-to-Knee Pose (Janu Sirsasana).

Put some red color (the color most associated with the root chakra) in your environment. Anoint a cloth with peppermint oil and take a whiff. Do a yoga squat. stand with legs a shoulder width apart and toes pointing slightly outward. Squat until your buttocks almost touch the floor and the knees are deeply bent but your spine remains straight. Place your elbows on the inner thighs and form the prayer mudra with your hands at your heart. Close your eyes. Breathe into the squat. Feel your Muladhara chakra open. Keep this stance for several cycles of breath and then sit in the Lotus or Half Lotus Pose and meditate on grounding energies.

RITUAL 126.
MAKE TIME FOR MORE SLEEP

CHANGE SLEEP PATTERNS
FOR A BETTER LIFE

Scientists say there are many reasons we don't get enough sleep—jet lag, eating and drinking too late, alcohol and coffee consumption, stress, electronic device lights blinking in the bedroom, sleep disorders, variable work shifts, and overreliance on sleep aids, among them. The body requires sufficient good sleep in order to repair itself. Less than the recommended seven to nine hours, and consequences start showing up—obesity, heart disease, memory issues, depression, and diabetes. A certain type of white blood cell known as a T-cell doesn't work as well to fight off infection when you are sleep deprived.

Sleep repairs frazzled nerves and helps you feel connected again to your core. When you get enough sleep, you wake up refreshed and energized. You have sharper mental acuity and heightened creativity. Start a new routine for feeling grounded before bed.

- Darken the room and make sure it's cool and quiet.
- Do not store electronic devices in the bedroom.
- Create a winding-down routine (such as yoga asanas that calm rather than excite).
- Keep to a regular schedule.
- Deep breathe for several cycles as you lie in bed.
- Say an affirmation such as "I welcome deep, restful sleep."

RITUAL 127.
USE THE ANCIENT CRYSTALS

Tap the Grounding
Power of Stones

Jet black onyx, hematite, and obsidian crystals share more than their dark color. These stones mined from the belly of the earth have an incredible power to ground you when you need it. Onyx, in particular, is favored by those who enjoy using crystals in their healing practices as an agent for strength against emotional upheaval. When you know you'll have to participate in an event that is going to push your emotional buttons, gather one or more of these stones and put them in your pocket. It's important that they be close to your body and that you can feel their weight, surfaces, and energies.

With any or all of these stones in your pocket, you get a sense of being grounded to the earth, so important during a stressful meeting with attorneys or bosses, or at a funeral of a beloved relative or a young colleague, or in a courtroom where you know there's going to be drama. Choose your stone for the occasion and carry it on your person in a place to which you have easy access (such as in a pocket). Hold it in your hand. Feel its power to ground. Obsidian is especially good for clarity. Hematite restores your sense of stability and grounding. Onyx brings calm to mental jitters. Each morning, hold the stone in your palm or roll it in your hand throughout the day in times of stress. Recite your favorite mantra until you feel anchored and peaceful.

RITUAL 128.
CREATE A PERSONALIZED YOGA RITUAL

Use It to Center and Ground

If you've been doing yoga for a while, you probably have discovered favorite asanas and sequences. For those times when you are feeling out of sorts or mentally agitated or have suffered a deep personal loss, get on your mat and start to work. Set an intention to let go of something, or to bring in something such as healing and calmness and tranquility. Start into the first asana with breathing that is deliberate, long, and slow on the inhalation and double the length on the exhalation.

Try the Cow Pose—get on all fours, knees directly below hips, elbows and shoulders perpendicular to the floor. Inhale and draw your buttocks and chest upward. Allow your tummy to sink downward. Lift and hold your head straight. On the exhale, move from this posture into the Cat Pose. Exhale. Arch your spine, and drop your head toward the floor. Inhale and come back to center. Next, move into the Extended Puppy Pose—still on your knees, but now you walk your arms forward along the floor, wrists in line with the shoulders, hips above the knees. Extend your arms straight out, palms down. Do this sequence or one you develop whenever you need to feel grounded.

RITUAL 129.
TAP INTO THOREAU'S
TONIC OF WILDERNESS

Find Your Grounding and Peace

Henry David Thoreau believed the cure for all that ails the world and the individual could be found in nature. For Thoreau, forays into the Maine woods, known as a wild and rugged area by the Penobscot Indians for thousands of years before him, provided a kind of peacefulness that could center and ground like perhaps nothing else. You don't have to take along a bateau (a type of boat Thoreau used) or even a tent and backpack if you don't plan to stay in the wild place of your choice. The important thing is to find some place in nature where you feel centered and connect with earth energies.

Nature will ground you when you leave behind the fast-paced world for a while. In the country or mountains or desert, time seems to slow down to a more natural rhythm. Sit and be mindful of all that your senses take in. Drink water. Roll up your pant legs; take off your shoes and socks. Run the bottoms of your feet over smooth stones or chill out in sparkling cold stream water. Let the subtle earth currents fill you with the tonic of wilderness. Feel grounded. Give thanks.

RITUAL 130.
SPEND QUALITY TIME IN A HAMMOCK

REST AND REWIND

Every now and then, breaking free from a hectic schedule can spark new creative thinking and bring new energy to your spiritual endeavors. In the islands of the world, hammocks are instruments of peace and tranquility. Strung from trees or posts anchored in concrete, these durable rope beds sway naturally in tropical breezes under shady tree canopies. Increasingly, people are hanging hammocks in their homes on hooks and anchors in the walls of a family room, a man cave, or a basement bonus area. Hammocks can be used as beds with an added bonus that they don't have to be made. They don't create pressure points on your body. You fall to sleep with a rocking motion that finds resonance with a mother rocking her infant. In a hammock you can feel grounded even as you catnap or dive deep into sleep.

Crawl into your hammock after lunch after you've spread out a blanket in it. Tuck a tiny travel pillow beneath your head. Feel cradled as if in a womb. Let the rocking motion lull your senses into quiet. Put your mindfulness there: "Breathing in, I draw in peace. Breathing out, I let go all negative energies."

RITUAL 131.
ACCEPT WHAT YOU CAN'T CHANGE

Focus on What You Can

Emotional upheaval can show up during any point in your life as a result of past emotional trauma, sudden changes, life-threatening illness, death of a loved one, a major move, or post-traumatic stress. You feel you are on a roller coaster of negative emotions and you can't get off. If the trauma relates to a past event, you might want to seek professional help, because probing the old wound likely will call up repressed emotions that can feel overpowering. Some of the emotions and reactions that can surface during an emotional upheaval include anger, anxiety, crying, dizziness, diarrhea, hyperventilation, and stomach tightness.

When psychological distress sets in as a result of some major life change, try to accept what you cannot change. Exercise can help temper the flood of unleashed brain chemicals and slow brain waves. Relaxation and meditation can be powerful grounding forces. When you are calm, you can determine the triggers to avoid. Wear your sandalwood japa mala beads around your neck as an anchoring force. Until the emotional storm passes, every hour touch the beads and affirm: "I am a child of the Universe, untouched by the upheavals in this world. Today I rest in the peace of my Soul's healing light."

RITUAL 132.
SEEK TO SPIRITUALLY GROUND YOURSELF

RELEASE UNWANTED ENERGIES

If you are a healer doing body work or just a dutiful parent who occasionally gives a massage to your spouse or your kids, you may unwittingly take on their energies. You may have symptoms such as feeling flighty, light-headed, shaky, and having the sensation of floating or feeling dazed and disconnected. Spiritual grounding or earthing can help restore your sense of connectedness to the earth.

- Run a salt bath of warm water with a cup of sea salt to cleanse, refresh, and ground you.
- Walk on a grassy lawn barefoot, releasing unwanted energies.
- Enjoy a piece of dark chocolate that's high in antioxidants, rich in stress-fighting minerals and soluble fiber, and contains anandamide, a lipid that activates your brain's sense of pleasure.
- Include root vegetables in your diet too. High in vitamins and minerals, root veggies grow underground and symbolize your natural deep connection with the earth.

After working with your patient or family member, wash your hands with soap and water. Arc your hands over your head by placing palm sides touching to make a hood and bring them down quickly to flick away unseen energy. Do this three times. Step out into fresh air and breathe deeply for several cycles to ground, refresh, and revitalize yourself.

RITUAL 133.
VISIT THE SEASHORE

WATCH WAVES

Sitting on the seashore and watching waves is not only mesmerizing, it can evoke that deep, eternal connection with ancient rhythms that can make you feel safe and secure. The waves steal silently into the shore, lap or crash, only to retreat again in an endless dance that's gone on for millions of years. Taking up a position on the sand in a dune or a rocky overlook where you can see the endless vista of an ocean can facilitate a sense of transformation and healing. Being in and around water rests your brain from overstimulation. You experience a soft fascination—alert and yet mindful, peaceful, and calm—a state referred to as a blue-mind state.

To inspire feelings of awe that you are connected to something far greater than yourself, take a shower with closed eyes and let the sound of water induce a blue-mind state. Stand under the pelting water and conceptualize the vastness of an ocean. Visualize aquamarine blue. Daydream. Feel an ancient connectedness with something as vast and powerful as the ocean. Let this feeling ground you.

RITUAL 134.
CHOOSE TO CUT YOUR LOSSES

LISTEN TO THE INNER VOICE

Sometimes when things are not going as you expected, it's better to cut your losses and move on than to hang on and deal with the stress, financial drain, emotional drag, and loss of time. Perhaps your issue is a relationship you've been trying to salvage for way too long, a business venture with an adversarial partner who isn't on the same page and doesn't share your vision for the company direction, or a renovation of a house that should have been a simple flip but became a money pit. Whatever it is, you've likely been overriding that soft intuitive voice telling you to cut your losses and move on—that the price you'll end up paying isn't worth it. Why would you want to stay invested in a losing battle?

If you have a situation where you feel overwhelmed by a shrinking pool of options to fix the problem you are facing, pick up a grounding stone such as obsidian. Put it in your pocket and touch it as you walk in nature. Let your thoughts wrap around what could happen if you just cut your losses. Chalk the experience up to lessons learned. Consider what you gain by letting go and moving on. It's surprisingly grounding.

RITUAL 135.
GET INSTANTLY ANCHORED

Use Mindfulness Practice Where You Are

Life can feel like a treadmill at times. In spite of wanting to jump off or slow the roll, you drink another coffee or energy beverage and keep on pushing yourself. Work is important. Getting kids to and from school has to be handled. Shopping for food, prepping meals, and doing the cleanup requires some time. There's laundry and homework. Your spouse or partner might help...or not. Somehow, you have to find time to exercise and enjoy your spiritual work, but squeezing it into an already packed day seems like an exercise in futility. You feel as flighty as a heritage chicken who just wants to fly away. What can you do to feel grounded, centered, and focused on the here and now?

Be mindful as you laugh at a joke. Notice all the sensations you feel. Laughter pulls you into the moment. Eat something healthy such as a spring roll. Chew it slowly, noticing how the texture and character of it changes as you chew. Pay attention to the flavor. Consider the nutritional value. Try mindfulness of your sense of place. Bring all your senses into this moment to inform you of the landscape in which you are anchored. When tired of the treadmill, step off for a moment. Take a seat. Rub your palms together. Fold them over your heart. Enter mindfulness. Be still and anchored in the present.

RITUAL 136.
SIT ON YOUR MAGIC CARPET

FIND GROUNDING ON THE GROUND

If you've been feeling like you are going to emotionally short-circuit, it's time to ground. You can feel better instantly by throwing a small carpet or blanket on the ground and taking a seat. Think of the things you can do on the carpet—read a book, have a picnic, color a mandala, do a tarot reading, play a game of chess, brush your dog, hand sew or knit, thread some beads, or make a dream catcher or a friendship bracelet. You might invite your kids or spouse or a friend to join you on the blanket. The point is to feel the earth supporting you and sending beneficial energies into you. You might find yourself running earth through your fingers. That's also a way to get the excitement, overthinking, overfeeling energy out of your body.

Notice the quality of your breathing—jagged, ragged, long, short, smooth, or easy. Next, get on your sitting bones and visualize roots spreading from you outward and downward, anchoring you. Lean forward to calm the parasympathetic nervous system. Feel centered. Slowed. Grounded.

RITUAL 137.
SHUT OUT THE SENSES

Explore Your Vast Interiority

In ancient yoga, there is a technique to close the ears and eyes and nose to shut off all sensory stimulation so that you can move your consciousness more deeply inward. There's a tremendous sense of power and connectedness as you leave behind the world of matter and turn inward to concentrate on the ever-expanding spiritual sphere. With all the static held back, you behold a vast interior world. In that place, you find your way home to the hearth of your being. You experience inner light, love, and spiritual happiness. In meditation, you find mysterious new thresholds to cross where you gain new insight, meaning, and wisdom.

Begin each day anew with the goal of exploring your inner landscape. Find a comfortable position on your sitting bones. Slip on a mask to cover your eyes. Put in earplugs or hold your ears shut with your fingers. Breathe through your mouth—not your nose, since you want the olfactory sense shut off. Turn your attention inward. Mentally affirm: "I am entering the temple of silence where I'm centered, supported, and nourished by the Infinite."

RITUAL 138.
SHARE FOOD

Put Meaning Back Into Meals

In the old days when families gathered to share a meal or break bread with friends, the event was infused with meaning, often starting with a prayer and then welcoming banter. Today, everyone eats in a hurry. Family members don't talk much or laugh together; in truth, in some homes people vent about their day over dinner...that is, if they sit down together at all. It's fast food and hurry, hurry.

If you want to recapture meaning for your meals, consider discussing with your family a ritual that includes showing up on time. To feel grounded in the here and now during mealtime, make a ritual of the following.

- Set out a meal on a clean tablecloth or place mats.
- Say a prayer of gratitude for the food and those who prepared it.
- Make a rule to leave smartphones and other devices in the other room.
- Ask everyone to use proper speech, manners, and good behavior.
- Share knowledge and otherwise enjoy the company of those around you.

RITUAL 139.
SPEND QUALITY TIME WITH MISS KITTY

LET YOUR CAT HELP YOU FIND YOUR CENTER

When you come home at the end of the day, your cat's meow does more than welcome you; it impacts your physical well-being. Regardless of experiences at work that might have frazzled your nerves or knocked you off balance, coming home to your little fur ball can help you feel grounded again. Within minutes, your mood gets boosted and calmness sets in as your level of cortisol (the stress hormone) goes down and serotonin (the feel-good hormone) increases. If that isn't reason enough to want to own a cat, consider that a twenty-year study showed that people who did not own a cat were 40 per cent more likely to die of a heart attack than people who did own a cat. Having a cat also benefits those suffering from depression.

Make it your ritual to spend time each day with your cat, giving and receiving unconditional love. Take notice of how you feel when you are centered and grounded as you groom your pet. In times of stress or other negative emotion, remember those positive feelings you experience when you are talking with your cat as you brush, feed, or groom her. Imagine feeling that way anytime external events trigger stress or other negative emotions in you.

RITUAL 140.
FINDING GROUNDING
IN YOUR HEART SPACE

ENTER THE FLOW

Anytime you stop and observe the flow of your breath, you momentarily abandon the ego-mind and return to the here and now. This is also known as the "I am" presence. During these moments of heightened awareness you can experience boundless freedom from all your troubles and instead embrace infinite possibility. You enter a higher vibration. Spend time in that moment of mindfulness and you enter a flow. Feeling a sense of gratitude for all you already have, you can intensify the magnetizing energy of your heart space, drawing to you more of what is good and beneficial for your life.

Connect with a moment of here and now through yoga and meditation. Sit in your favorite asana. Cross your hands over your heart. Feel the flow of your breath. Drain energy from your tailbone into the earth. Draw energy in from your crown. Consider what the body needs to feel balanced, grounded, and centered. Listen deeply to your voice of intuition. Use the power of visualization to feel the interconnectedness to all things. Be anchored in the never-ending flow of this moment. Feel grateful.

ROOTS FOR GROUNDING

- Become treelike in balance and equanimity.
- Visualize the taproot of your being connecting to earth energies.
- Root yourself in the practice of silence.

GROUNDING THROUGH CHAKRAS, SLEEP, AND STONES

- Stabilize the energies of your root chakra.
- Get more sleep.
- Work with grounding crystals.

GROUNDING ACTIVITIES

- Connect your feet with the earth.
- Rock rhythmically in a hammock.
- Commune with the ancient sea or sources of water.

GROUNDING BY LETTING GO

- Cut your losses.
- Drop anchor where you are.
- Shut out sensory stimulation.

GROUNDING THROUGH FOOD AND HEART ENERGIES

- Share a healthy meal.
- Love your pet.
- Find grounding through your heart.

Chapter 9

RITUALS FOR A RENEWED YOU

We are responsible for the construction of our lives. When our days make us feel as if we're in a mindless, empty rut and life isn't the exciting adventure it once was, just the right ritual can pull you into a different mindset, open your vision to the world, and propel you into new experiences. Renewal is something that anyone can bring about in any moment. You might pick up a self-help book that has a message for you that resonates with your desire to renew. Or, while watching a podcast, you enjoy a talk by a guest who frames some old concept in a new way. Or, on a weekend retreat with your church group, you reconnect with old friends and realize that values you used to believe in have fallen along the wayside.

Never feel that you can't get unstuck. Sometimes it just takes clearing out of old energy to make way for new circulation to happen. Maybe it's time to put meaning back into your life with some renewal rituals. Or consider joining a vision quest to birth a new vision for your life. Alternatively, you might take a long rest—as in vacation—and rethink the paradigm of your life. Whatever it takes, choose change. Move outside your comfort zone. Grow and evolve.

RITUAL 141.
GET YOUR WILD ON

Invite Your Inner Child to Play

Sometimes you just have to let your hair down and have some fun if you're stuck in a rut and can't figure out how to bust out. We were all children once. Somewhere deep inside you is the inner child you long ago forgot about. Invite him or her out to play. Do what used to make you happy. Was it painting, kicking a soccer ball around, or dancing in front of the sliding glass door where you could see your image? Perhaps you were the kind of child who loved manipulating Play-Doh, calculating hopscotch squares, jumping rope, playing a musical instrument, or drawing for hours under a tree. Or maybe you were the type who liked to climb them. Find that wild child again.

Afraid someone might see you? Forget about it. Find an old Hula-Hoop. Put it around your waist and start swerving in circles. Stretch out your arms. Whirl and twirl. Close your eyes. Peek out every now and again to avoid colliding with a bush or tree. Enjoy the movement. Feel young. Feel renewed. It's exhilarating.

RITUAL 142.
MAKE A PROFOUND CHOICE

HEAD OFF IN A NEW DIRECTION

Whether it's choosing a life partner, accepting a job on the other side of the world, or embarking on a new career path, such a time of profound choice will necessarily involve reflection, gestation, and cogitation. When you reach the momentous occasion in life when you are faced with a life-altering choice, take notice of how important and powerful that moment feels. Weighing all the pros and cons is one part of the learning curve. As you gain ideas and insights, you may also pinpoint concerns or details needing further attention. Your choice in part means reinventing yourself. It will be a new you interacting in the world in a new way. You might feel more exhilarated than ever before. Enjoy the ride.

Take pen and paper in hand. Write out the choice facing you and draw a circle around it. Call upon your Higher Self's wisdom through the voice of intuition to guide you as you draw spokes outward from the circle in a mind-mapping exercise to bring clarity. Let your excitement infuse the process as you make balloons and write the positives in them and boxes in which you write the negatives. Step back and look at the clear picture that's emerging. Feel gratitude.

RITUAL 143.
LOOK TO MAKE A MAJOR OVERHAUL

Start with Small Adjustments

You're ready to dissolve a partnership that hasn't worked in a while. The decision is major. It will radically shift your income, since you plan to buy out your partner's investment in the company and restructure when she is gone. You've known for a while you were going to do it; you just put it off until you felt the timing was right. So you've arrived at the now-or-never state. It's a big, scary step, but tackling it in some incremental adjustments removes fear and internal pressure. Put your creative hat on and push out the old brain fog. Pump up your energy and roll up your shirtsleeves. Write it all out on paper. See it as two processes. One is ending the relationship of two. The other is the restructure. Tackle the ending first with some breath work and a powerful visualization.

Light a stick of lavender incense for clarity. Breathe in and out five times, making the inhalation half as long as the exhalation. Close your eyes. Feel the increased mental energy. Visualize signing the dissolution agreement and shaking hands with your partner. Be mindful, noticing what new information comes up around feelings of renewal.

RITUAL 144.
STOP PLOWING OLD GROUND

ABANDON THE PAST

A surefire way to stay stuck is to keep plowing the same furrow or digging the same deep hole. The biggest problem people have with getting stuck and finding it difficult to move on is that they get hung up on something in the past; in moments that have already been lived. Perhaps they suffered a traumatic event, such as the shock of early success that ended up failing due to a nasty divorce or the cheating actions of a deceptive partner. Past failures must not dictate future business outcomes. The best and most successful businesspeople often point to past failures from which they learned incrementally and applied what they learned to ensure future successes. If you're stuck, you have to stop plowing the old ruts. Get moving mentally and physically.

To get a fresh perspective and shift into a new direction, eat some healthy food and get some regular exercise. You want new chemicals flowing into your brain to spark your creative imagination. That's the way to jump-start renewal.

- Go for a walk in the park and greet the sunrise.
- Make the prayer mudra at your heart.
- Affirm: "Welcome, Surya, Dispeller of Darkness. Bless me with your light."
- Visualize a shower of inner light sparking myriad ideas for new creative directions in your life.
- Whisper your thanks.

RITUAL 145.
STEAM AWAY YOUR OLD SELF

USE HERBS AND SCENTED OILS

Water is the great purifier. If you can't swim out a mile in the warm Ionian Sea or Caribbean Sea to soothe away your cares and feel revitalized, you can still find renewal in a steam bath with herbs and scented oils. The ancient Indian herb tulsi, also known as holy basil, can be combined with organic rose petals in a bag and added to your bath for a rejuvenating experience. In the ancient Ayurveda, herbs that rejuvenate are known as medhya rasayana or nervines because they help calm the mind and relax the body. Diffuse some fragonia oil, since it is believed to be beneficial for harmonizing body-mind-spirit. Try mixing your own herbal concoction with your favorite oils and scents for body massaging after a rejuvenating bath.

In a glass container, mix together equal parts (2 ounces each) argan, jojoba oil, rose seed oil, and coconut oil. Place three drops of rose-geranium oil, six drops of frankincense oil, and add eight to ten drops of lavender oil. Shake and store in the fridge. Ritually apply after your bath.

RITUAL 146.
CULTIVATE NEW FRIENDS

BRING NEW MEANING INTO YOUR LIFE

Perhaps you'd like to become more assertive, less critical, or more forgiving. Or you'd like to pursue a new management style or try a radical approach to a creative project. Maybe you'd like to dive deeper into a particular spiritual discipline to derive more meaning. If you've read books on self-renewal, found them helpful, but still seek more insight, you might benefit from cultivating new knowledge and friends to bring new meaning to your life.

Each day, deep breathe, ground, and center yourself. Light sage to clear the space of any negative energy. Close your eyes. Conduct a self-examination of your qualities, traits, and habits to determine what you want to change. Or think about the new knowledge or friendships you'd like to acquire. After this daily meditative period, take a walk in nature and think about how you can start the process of change, which will undoubtedly involve more steps. Perhaps you could take or teach a class—a surefire way to meet new people and learn new information. Consider seeking out a mentor, counselor, or guru. At work, you might befriend the new guy or girl by starting a meaningful conversation. When you feel a strong connection with someone, suggest continuing your conversation over tea or coffee. Know the renewal process has begun.

RITUAL 147.
SHAKE THINGS UP

Renew with the New Moon

The lunar cycle brings a new moon every month (sometimes two new moons). This period is the perfect time to release old patterns of thinking, things that no longer serve a purpose, and fears that impede your personal advancements and spiritual growth. It's the time to clear away clutter. If you've been putting off a health checkup for fear of bad news or starting a gym routine that requires a daily workout or a financial reassessment after a bad tax year, find the fortitude to start anew. Shaking things up in your life can stimulate movement, momentum, and growth.

On the new moon (renewal time) of every month, do the following ritual. Work from intention. Clean your personal space and then use cypress, juniper, or lavender essential oil in a diffuser to clear negative energies from your space. Spend time in meditation considering what thoughts, fears, or guilt you might mentally be holding on to that impedes your well-being and spiritual growth. Release these. Then, after meditation, get to work releasing physical items in your life that no longer serve any purpose.

RITUAL 148.
CLEAR THE CLUTTER

Renew Your Environment

You moved into your house years ago and every year you bring in new things. However, you don't take a lot away. Pretty soon, you've got a house full of stuff you're storing and never use. Begin the process of renewal by clearing the clutter. If you feel overwhelmed, choose one area to tackle—maybe the garage, the attic, a bedroom that's no longer being used as sleeping quarters. Get out your boxes—one for donation, one for things needing repair, and one for items you want to keep. Start in one area of the room and work your way around. When you've filled the donation box, take it to the car and start another box. At the end of the day, take those boxes straight to a hospice center, a thrift store, a shelter, or a service organization. When your space is clear, you'll feel energy on a palpable level moving through the space.

Once a month, do a ritual clutter clearing. Put on some happy music. Set out bottles of water to stay hydrated while you work. Get the boxes to assemble, the roller and tapes, and packing paper. Enjoy the process of renewing your space and reclaiming your life.

RITUAL 149.
DO THE UNEXPECTED

Dance in the Moonlight

If you want to feel alive and intensely rejuvenated, get a little crazy. Do something spontaneous such as having a picnic (even in the front yard) or doing a totally out of the ordinary activity such as dancing under the light of the full moon or lying on fresh powder and making a snow angel. Maybe you take a day off and visit an architectural salvage yard, spend an afternoon antiquing, or take the subway to the end of the line just because you can. If it's springtime, go buy a packet of seeds for a butterfly garden and scatter them in a raked bed. Or ride the rails somewhere. If it's fall, make a pumpkin pie from scratch using a sugar pumpkin you buy at the farmers' market.

Whatever is out of the ordinary for you, give it a shot. You'll find youthful exuberance taking over and replacing the humdrum routine that might be bogging down your days. Make it a weekly ritual to focus on a period of deep breathing. Bring your mindfulness into your heart space. Hold a pink crystal there as you focus your thoughts on something fun and fresh and different to do. Say an intention: "Today I intend to experience the world with joy and childlike wonder." Then, go and do it.

RITUAL 150.
DEVELOP AN EXPECTANT MINDSET

TRUST YOUR BEST LIFE
IS TAKING SHAPE

You don't have to wait to map out a new life for renewal to happen. Adjust your thinking in this moment, right now. Your intention to renew goes right into the energy matrix of the Universe and a shift begins. Hold on to your expectation that things will change because you want them to change and they will. Form an intention, do visualizations, write out a few positive affirmations, take some actions in which you create a new lifestyle for the new you, cultivate gratitude, and trust and expect your best life ever is already on its way to you. You won't know exactly when or how, but change is coming. You can count on it.

Hold in your hands a piece of amethyst, a purple-colored quartz stone that brings serenity and rebalancing. It also clears negativity from your space, so it's good to keep a tall geode of the dark purple crystal in the bedroom. It will bring in new energy. Place your amethyst in the northeast corner of your home, the area of self-cultivation and spiritual growth. If you are experiencing turbulent emotional times, keep a piece of tumbled amethyst in your pocket to touch for healing and calming and grounding.

RITUAL 151.
INVEST IN A NEW HOBBY

Make Sure It's Thought Stimulating

Is a new hobby calling out to you? If so, consider how you might use an interest in a new activity to not only renew your spirit but benefit your brain. Scientific studies have shown that hobbies such as reading, puzzle solving, and letter writing may help stave off symptoms of dementia, including memory loss. Even if there are disease changes already taking place in your brain, scientists say keeping your brain active and involved apparently helps keep certain brain circuits working effectively.

Scientists believe people who have greater memory, thinking, and learning capabilities somehow are able to delay the onset of symptoms of Alzheimer's disease and other dementias. Consider a hobby that requires you to puzzle through problems, or learn a new language, or how to play a musical instrument. Every evening after a long day of work, start your ritual by putting on a piece of music that lifts your spirit. Sit down and close your eyes. Breathe in and out deeply six times. Then chant the words, "Om, shanti, shanti, shanti." Repeated three times, *shanti* (which means peace) is generally taken to mean peace in body, mind, and spirit or the whole being. Recite the mantra before tackling your chosen hobby or activity to stimulate your brain cells.

RITUAL 152.
PUT SOME OPTIMISM IN
YOUR LIFE WITH A RITUAL

EMPOWER IT

If you are not a naturally optimistic person who sees the proverbial cup half-full instead of half-empty, there are some things you can do to cultivate more optimism and renew your spirit. Live one day at a time, as though it was all you had. You can't worry about the past or the future. Put everything you've got into this single day and notice how your attitude shifts. Chase the rainbows in your life and shake off negative thinking. Surround yourself with friends who have positive energy and optimistic thoughts. Laugh out loud at every opportunity. Your natural state is one of joy, not glumness. Join an optimist club through Optimist International, an organization that fosters optimism through its creed and its work in communities of the world.

Form an intention to feel and reflect more optimism in your life. Light a jasmine candle for optimism. Write yourself a note with a sunny, smiley face on it that states: "I am a ray of light, spreading joy and optimism wherever I go to whomever I meet." Place a thin, loose rubber band around your wrist. As you go through your day, flick the band to remind you of your commitment to optimism.

RITUAL 153.
ASK THREE FRIENDS TO KIDNAP YOU

Have a Little Fun

If you've ever had a friend show up unexpectedly and whisk you away for an afternoon of fun, you know how refreshed, exhilarated, and renewed that can make you feel. Why wait for your friends to get the idea that you need a break from the doldrums of your daily grind? Call them up and explain this is your plan to feel renewed. Maybe one or more of them also needs a break. Go wine-tasting or catch the latest artsy film at the local theater. Take a picnic lunch to the beach or pack up some sandwiches and water and head out to a farm to pick local produce. If crafting is your thing, ask your friends to sign up the group at a local pottery painting shop or take a beadmaking class together.

If you enjoy your day, why not make it a monthly foray into the unknown? Let each friend choose a secret destination and activity each month. To stimulate your creative imagination for other ideas of fun outings, put on some happy music. Get out a notebook. Jot down your name along with your friends'. Beneath each one, list activities you know they love to do.

RITUAL 154.
ORGANIZE A GROUP

Focus on Your Passion

A quick way to turn your life around and move in a new direction is to focus on your passion. Involving others means you'll keep your attention on the work of the organization and stay focused. If some life event has sparked your passion for something—be it clean air or water, animal rights, human rights, eco-travel, organic winemaking, or something else—consider how you might create a movement or at least an organization to promote interest in your idea.

Upon awakening, when your mind is refreshed from sleep, set aside time to do some mindful breathing. Begin meditating on ideas for a new life direction. Focus on what speaks powerfully to your heart. Can you develop a vision for a long-range project that addresses your strongest passion? If so, what might be some of the action steps to create an organization that addresses your keen interest? Write down your ideas in a journal. Focus on the meaning they bring to your life and why you'd want to spend weeks, months, even years involved in the work of a group that shares your zeal. When you feel your head and heart are aligned around your vision, write out the steps to begin to actualize it.

RITUAL 155.
SLIP AWAY FOR A COUPLES RETREAT

HARNESS INTENTION FOR
A BETTER RELATIONSHIP

Putting the spark back into your relationship with your spouse can feel like a new beginning. Women live in their hearts and heads. They primarily express love through their emotions while guys may generally express love through acts of doing. Understanding this difference can help you and your partner build new bridges to each other. When you tell him you feel sad that you don't share your feelings like you did when you were first married, he might feel bad and want to fix it, but his fix won't be talking through every nuance of what emotions you might have or are feeling. If you're looking for validation and affirmation that you are right and you want him to behave differently, you might have to just get over that.

Instead, plan a long weekend or weeklong retreat where you two are captive audiences for each other. On the retreat, undertake the following suggested steps as a daily ritual for as long as your retreat lasts. First, hold hands, walk and talk, and freely express your most intimate selves to each other. Fly-fish or ride horseback with him in the woods or do some other fun activity. Guys like activities with their talking. Pledge your desire to draw closer and formulate a plan with your partner for how the two of you will do that. Talk about your plan again before bed.

RITUAL 156.
MAKE A DAY OF FORGIVENESS

LET GO OF PAST PAIN

Wipe the slate clean and start anew—that's one way to feel renewal in your life. Judaism has its Day of Atonement (Yom Kippur) in which believers look back over the past year and evaluate their transgressions. Seeking forgiveness, they formulate an intention to make things right between them and God and each other. Desiring health and happiness in the coming year, they do penance and ask forgiveness so that they can let go of past hurts that they have either suffered or inflicted on others. You can put this ancient sacred practice to work for you. Allocate a day once a month during which you spend time in reflection. Use the time to examine your life and try to understand how you might cultivate a different way of thinking and behaving that would better serve you and your community.

Burn some sandalwood incense to cleanse and consecrate your sacred space. Light a white candle. Sit straight with eyes closed and your focus on deep in and out breaths. When you feel centered, confess your transgressions, ask for forgiveness, and let go.

RITUAL 157.
CONTEMPLATE DEATH

EMBRACE LIFE

His Holiness the Fourteenth Dalai Lama advocated that you should be mindful of death as a way to appreciate the gift of life you've been given. There's nothing so clarifying about the preciousness of life as the surety of death. No one escapes death. It is an ancient repetitive cycle of nature. All who are born will die. In the West, we tend to avoid talking about death until it touches our lives through a family member, friend, celebrity or political figure, or a personal hero.

From birth, you are marching toward your end. For many, that means they can blissfully skip through life and not really value what a spectacular gift human birth is. In the Tibetan view, death is a concept. It ceases to exist once gross consciousness and the physical body are released. While many might see the exercise of thinking about death as a morbid activity, in truth it gives a deeper appreciation for what you have and might inspire you to do more with the life you've got. Designate one day of the week or certain days of every month for a ritual meditation on life and death. Each time you undertake this meditation, begin the ritual with mindful breath work to feel centered and grounded. Withdraw into the temple of your heart. Call upon the Universe to bless you with a presence that holds you in peace, safety, and love as you invite thoughts around your end time.

RITUAL 158.
SHIFT PERSONAL SPACE ENERGY

OPEN INNER SPACE

It's been said that you can tell how organized a person's life is by looking at his or her room. If your room is wall-to-wall clutter, books piled high from the floor, clothes lying in piles or boxes, and the bed isn't made, you might feel just as disorganized in your life. Do you know where your work clothes are located? Are clean clothes mixed in with the dirty? Can you find two shoes that match? Can you even find your wallet or your car key?

If some of that scenario speaks to you, it's time to create inner and outer space. Start tackling that room. Get some plastic containers with lockable lids. Start picking up and organizing. Purchase a small file cabinet or get some stacking Bankers Boxes to organize your files. Hang a rack of key hooks on the wall. Wash, dry, fold, or hang your clothing. Close the closet doors. Move in a plant to bring oxygen to your room. First thing each day, make it a ritual to make your bed and put away your clothes. Notice how clearing the clutter makes you feel more in control and creates more spaciousness in your consciousness.

RITUAL 159.
LET GO OF WHY

Face What Is

When there is some senseless act that touches our lives, it's a natural human trait to want to make some kind of sense out of the tragedy. Why did the tornado sweep through your community, taking down your church and school and bank? How will your town ever recover? Or why was the only house that slid down in the mudslide your home? You lost everything. Why? Or why did the hurricane destroy fifteen homes on one street and leave the streets behind and in front untouched? Asking why isn't nonsensical but the truth is sometimes the why of something just can't be known.

When a natural disaster hits, there is usually a scientific explanation. But it won't answer the *why me* question. Clergy members might say that the why is for a higher power, not humans, to know. For a situation that feels like total cataclysm, the best option is to accept the situation as it is. You'll be forced to begin anew. Make it a ritual each day to start the day with an affirmation: "I am determined to find strength and resiliency in every moment of my day as I start my life over."

RITUAL 160.
CULTIVATE SELF-LOVE

Renew Daily

Self-love is compassion and caring for the self; it's not "all about me." Self-love is action that includes behaviors and attitudes that you cultivate in order to better appreciate yourself. Society is always screaming messages that you have to do more, be more, give more. Forget about the accomplishments you haven't achieved yet. Instead, focus on the lovely, unique being that you are. Give attention to what nourishes your spiritual, psychological, and emotional growth. Nurture yourself through daily care of your body-mind-spirit needs.

That means caring for your body through good nutrition and hydration, adequate sleep, exercise, and healthy intimacies and relationships with others. Self-love demands that you protect yourself from harmful energies of those who do not respect your boundaries. To cultivate caring toward yourself, forgive and let go of guilt. You don't benefit from having guilt in your life, and being hard on yourself won't further your happiness or success. Love yourself and live an intentional life on purpose with your deepest dreams and desires. Make it a ritual to rise each day and affirm that this is a new day, full of possibilities. Claim it as yours.

CHANGE YOUR MINDSET

- Foster feelings of childlike wonder.
- Cultivate optimism.
- Develop a sense of expectancy.

SHAKE THINGS UP

- Choose a new life direction.
- Envision an overhaul in increments.
- Abandon the past.
- Take a steam bath.

CREATE MOVEMENT

- Make more inner space by clearing the clutter around you.
- Do something completely unexpected.
- Take up a new hobby

GO DEEP

- Stop asking why and embrace what is.
- Befriend end-of-life issues.
- Cultivate self love.

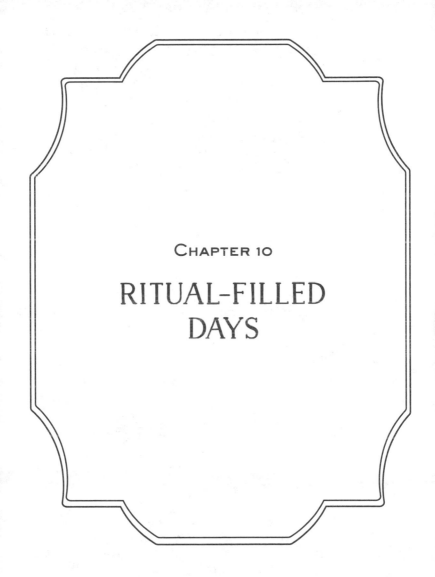

CHAPTER 10

RITUAL-FILLED DAYS

Living at the speed of modern life, you may feel you are simply going through the motions, living your life in reflex, conditioned to respond repetitively to triggers instead of making mindful choices to empower every area of your existence. As you rush toward unknown landscapes and the distant boundaries of your life, you can become disoriented and lose that sense of childlike wonder that life is nothing short of miraculous and sacred. You forget to notice the presences around you—the energy of a flower, the diligence of a bee, the gentle countenance of the face of your partner or spouse, the generosity of a total stranger, the soulful eyes of your master or yoga teacher, and the powerful presences in meditation and prayer.

Your life takes on meaning when you do rituals, whether in groups, as a couple, or alone. Instead of breezing through your days without much thought about when they might come to an end or living in ways of rote repetition and reaction, obsessed with acquiring like a dutiful consumer, you can choose to live more wisely and meaningfully with a spiritual consciousness. Rituals make it easy.

APPLY RITUAL TO HEALTH

When your mental and physical health is threatened by chronic stress or illness, try rituals for a healthier you. You might have unwittingly violated the laws of nature through unhealthy habits that create imbalance and disease. Restore your body's natural well-being through rituals of good nutrition, proper hydration, exercise, and deep and restful sleep.

Choose a daily ritual to work with when you want to emphasize a particular area of your life such as health and well-being. **Relish the Rainbow** (Ritual 6) might be a good daily ritual to start with, since nutrition is such an important factor in good health. Add the ritual of **Savor Sublime Green Tea** (Ritual 19), since it's recommended that you drink four cups a day to get green tea's benefits. Practice, too, daily rituals of hygiene such as **Do a Ritual Scrape** (Ritual 14) and **Keep Your Gut Healthy** (Ritual 17) to keep your microbiome in balance.

Once a week, you might add ecotherapy to your health regimen and **Book an Ayurvedic Massage** (Ritual 22). Then, once a month, do **Sniff a Memory** (Ritual 4) meditation and rebalance your chakras with the ritual **Use Bija Seed Sounds** (Ritual 5).

FOCUS ON A MORE EMPOWERED YOU

Perhaps your greatest desire is to get on purpose with your life, but you're unsure of how to embark on that process. To unlock your inner greatness, choose a daily ritual such as **Find Your Inner Power** (Ritual 23) or **Cultivate Your Inner Magnificence** (Ritual 24). Try chanting to draw into your being more confidence and a happier emotional state. If there are times when stagnation threatens to dampen the sparks of creativity within you or throw a shroud of deathly ordinariness over your life, you can choose to shift into a higher vibration through a chanting ritual that fosters transformation, such as **Use Bija Seed Sounds** (Ritual 5). Add a weekly practice of linking with the Divine through your senses. Turn inward with a ritual to **Recognize Your Unique Gifts** (Ritual 52). Then, once a month, do the ritual of **Embark on a Personal Retreat** (Ritual 54).

TAP INTO A MORE PEACEFUL YOU

When your body-mind system is healthy and you feel more empowered, you might find yourself longing for extended periods of peace. Incorporate daily rituals to invoke and experience the deep relief and healing powers of peace. Incorporate into your day the rituals of **Practice Loving-Kindness Toward Yourself** (Ritual 47) and **Deflect White Noise Damage** (Ritual 48). Once a week, invoke the ritual of sitting in holy silence through the ritual of **Recognize Your Unique Gifts**

(Ritual 52). On a monthly or bimonthly basis, plan on listening to a guided meditation app and **Make Time for Meditation** (Ritual 59) and **Find Peace Through Self-Acceptance** (Ritual 60).

CULTIVATE A MORE PROSPEROUS YOU

Between the poles of feeling prosperous and not having prosperity are infinite possibilities. Through the ritual of intention and gratitude, you can live more abundantly and have more financial prosperity in your life. Shift the stale energy of prosperity to open the flow, bringing more of what you want, through two powerful rituals—**Eliminate Thoughts of Lack** (Ritual 61) and **Write a Blessings List** (Ritual 62). Use tools such as those listed in **Spray a Scent of Success** (Ritual 63) and **Attract Abundance with Citrine** (Ritual 64). Once each week, add a new ritual such as **Imprint Your Subconscious** (Ritual 66) and **Keep Money Circulating in Your Orbit** (Ritual 67). As the energy of prosperity continues to open and bring its gifts to you, do a monthly ritual of **Get Out Your Checkbook** (Ritual 69) and write yourself a check. A couple of other monthly activities might include **Pursue Inner Wealth** (Ritual 74) and **Nurture Others Toward Their Greatness** (Ritual 77). When welcoming abundance becomes the norm, you likely will feel grateful and inspired to give back. Check out the chapter on gratitude (Chapter 6) for rituals for how to do that.

EXPRESS A MORE GRATEFUL YOU

When you want to have a more grateful (and thus, happier) life, a good daily habit is to record what abundance is already yours to claim. This is akin to counting your blessings. A good ritual to start with is **Keep a Gratitude Journal** (Ritual 83). This launches you on a path of seeing the goodness that is flowing into your life already. Then you easily transition to making gratitude a daily guiding principle of your life through the ritual of **Sow Seeds of Gratitude** (Ritual 84), starting with those you love. Another daily ritual is **Pray Often** (Ritual 90) and also **Show Gratitude Through Ahimsa** (Ritual 86). Once a week, do a thoughtful ritual of expressing your gratitude through a personal communication—**Write a Letter** (Ritual 88); **Put Up a Bounty of Gratitude Jar** (Ritual 95); and **Hang a Whiteboard with Pens** (Ritual 98). Take time monthly to read through the notes in the jar and on the whiteboard. Let them inspire you to even stronger feelings of gratitude.

GET IN TOUCH WITH A MORE INTENTIONAL YOU

Precise language counts when it comes to making your desires known to the Universe. Get started now declaring your intentions for today, tomorrow, and the future life you envision. On a daily basis, review the first ritual on **Learn to Be Precise** (Ritual 101) so you'll know how to phrase intentions for your desires. Then follow up and **Seize Opportunity When It Shows Up** (Ritual 102). If you're looking for love, reread the ritual for **Find True Love** (Ritual 104) and give some attention to this ritual on a weekly basis **Getting Along Better with Others** (Ritual 114) might signal an important shift so that you can open the way for a new romantic person to enter your life. Each month, utilize the advice in **Create Better Karma** (Ritual 116). The beginning or end of the month is also a good time to **Bring Light to Your Entrepreneurial Desire** (Ritual 118). As you work with intention and the universal law of attraction, you'll discover your life shifting in new directions as you open yourself to the realm of infinite possibility and become a cocreator with the Divine of every aspect of your life.

GET GROUNDED WHEN YOU NEED BALANCE

When life's challenges come at you faster than is comfortable for you to handle, stop and breathe your way back to mindfulness and balance. Review and practice the techniques in **Retreat Into the Practice of Mouna** (Ritual 123) and then **Anchor Yourself** (Ritual 124) in a mindful moment. These two rituals could become your daily refuge. When you feel the need for more grounding as you move into your day, review **Use the Ancient Crystals** (Ritual 127). Do yoga asanas such as **Become the Tree Root** (Ritual 121) and visualizations such as those found in the ritual **Touch Your Taproot** (Ritual 122). As you gain relief from these daily practices, consider formulating a yoga sequence of asanas that you can take your time doing each week to ensure you remain balanced and grounded. **Create a Personalized Yoga Ritual** (Ritual 128) can benefit your work on other issues while you spend time on your mat. Find time each week to bond with your pet. See **Spend Quality Time with Miss Kitty** (Ritual 139) for suggestions of how your pet can help you ground and center yourself. Plan a monthly grounding retreat—**Visit the Seashore** (Ritual 133) or **Tap Into Thoreau's Tonic of Wilderness** (Ritual 129).

BIRTH A RENEWED YOU

If you aren't satisfied with the way things are currently going, use the power of intention to shift your life in new directions. If you can imagine it and visualize it, you can make it happen. Supercharge your dream with emotion as if you already have brought that dream into reality and you will be birthing a new you in no time. Renewal doesn't have to be complicated; in fact, it can be as simple as child's play. You just have to **Get Your Wild On** (Ritual 141) and choose to move forward. Find some ideas in **Make a Profound Choice** (Ritual 142). You can do these rituals every day and find something new in them along with **Stop Plowing Old Ground** (Ritual 144). Once a week, take a nice, long steam bath with herbs to help you **Steam Away Your Old Self** (Ritual 145). Then embrace activities that bring new friends and experiences into your orbit and **Slip Away for a Couples Retreat** (Ritual 155) or **Organize a Group** (Ritual 154) or **Ask Three Friends to Kidnap You** (Ritual 153). On a monthly basis, devote some spiritual time to thinking about forgiveness and the end of life. See **Make a Day of Forgiveness** (Ritual 156) and also **Contemplate Death** (Ritual 157) to embrace a renewed appreciation for your precious gift of life. Impart more meaning into your life through your daily, weekly, and monthly ritual practice. Turn some love back in on yourself and cherish this human birth. Make your life blessed and worthwhile.

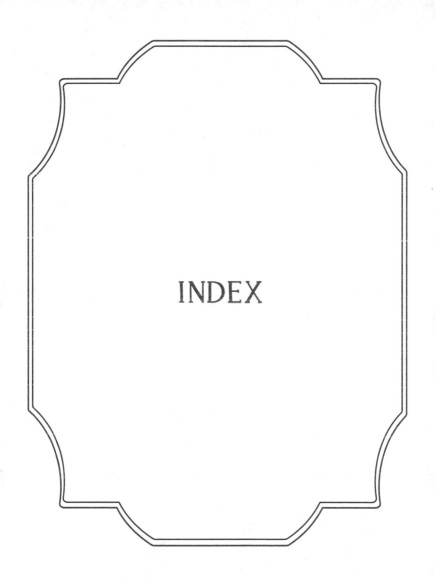

INDEX

ABOUT THE AUTHOR

Meera Lester, an internationally published author and world traveler, has written nearly thirty books, including *My Pocket Meditations*, *Sacred Travels*, *The Everything® Law of Attraction Book*, and *The Secret Power of You* (Adams Media) as well as mysteries. Since spending time in India and Nepal in her early twenties, she has been a devoted practitioner of hatha yoga, dhyana meditation, and kundalini maha yoga. She blogs from MeeraLester.com and HennyPennyFarmette.com.